# BRNO TRAVEL GUIDE

Engrossing tour to Brno's rich history, beautiful
architecture, cultural riches, and scenic
surroundings.

Edith M.scott

1

*Table of contents*

# 1 INTRODUCTION OF BRNO

The South Moravian Region contains Brno, the second-largest city in the Czech Republic. It is located where the Svratka and Svitava rivers meet and serve as the region's capital. Brno, which has a population of about 400,000, is a flourishing and cultural city renowned for its extensive history, stunning architecture, and active arts scene.

The history of the city dates back to the Paleolithic era. Numerous cultures, notably the Celts, Romans, and Slavs, have influenced it. Brno has historically played a significant role as a political, economic, and cultural hub in Central Europe.

Brno has an interesting mix of medieval, Gothic, Renaissance, and modernist architectural styles. Beautiful landmarks may be found in the city center, including the Cathedral of St. Peter and Paul, a recognizable image of Brno, and the imposing Spilberk Castle, a fortification that commands sweeping views of the city.

Brno is renowned for its thriving cultural scene in addition to its historical features. There are many museums, galleries, theaters, and music venues throughout the city, serving a variety of interests. The Summer Shakespeare Festival and the famed Ignis Brunensis Fireworks Competition are just a couple of the festivities that are held there throughout the year.

There are several parks and other green areas in Brno as well, offering opportunities for leisurely outdoor activity. The biggest park in the city, Luzanky Park, has nicely designed gardens, walking trails, and entertainment areas.

Brno is also a significant academic hub with several universities and research institutions. The most distinguished of them all is Masaryk University, which is renowned around the world for the caliber of its research and instruction. A robust scientific and technological environment has been cultivated by the city's strong emphasis on education and innovation.

The economy of Brno is strong and supported by several sectors, including the production of automobiles, machinery, electronics, and information technology. The city is known as a center for innovation and entrepreneurship and has drawn several multinational corporations. It is home to many business and technology parks, promoting cooperation and opening up job opportunities.

Brno has grown in popularity as a destination for tourists looking for an authentic Czech experience away from the busy masses of Prague due to its pleasant and welcoming atmosphere. Brno has much to offer for every visitor, whether they are interested in history, culture, architecture, or simply trying the local cuisine and nightlife.

A charming city, Brno combines a rich historical past with contemporary energy. Its importance in terms of culture, education, and the economy has made it a vibrant center in the middle of Europe. Brno provides visitors from all over the world with a distinctive and unforgettable experience because of its architectural treasures, vibrant academic environment, and numerous attractions.

This review sets the basis for further investigation of this intriguing city by looking for the charm and fascination of Brno.

1a. **Brno's history**

the history of Brno in brief:
Brno has a lengthy and colorful past that goes back to the Stone Age. Celtic tribes lived in the region where

Brno is today in the first century BC. Later, during the Roman era, a trade route known as the Amber Road that connected the Adriatic Sea with the Baltic Sea went through the region.

Brno joined the Great Moravian Empire, a Slavic empire that existed from the ninth to the tenth centuries, in the ninth century. During this period, the area prospered, and Brno developed into a significant commercial and cultural hub.

Brno joined the developing Czech state in the eleventh century and had a major influence on the creation of the Czech people. It developed into a royal metropolis and a significant regional political and economic center.

Brno had multiple wars and invasions over the years. Various troops, including the Swedes during the Thirty Years' War in the seventeenth century, occupied it.

During this time, the city sustained substantial damage, but it recovered and rebuilt.

Brno underwent industrialization and modernization in the 19th century, becoming a significant industrial hub in the Austro-Hungarian Empire. The textile, engineering, and manufacturing sectors of the city prospered and supported its economic development.

Due to political events, Brno underwent considerable changes in the 20th century. Brno joined the newly created Czechoslovakia in 1918 at the end of World War I and the collapse of the Austro-Hungarian Empire. In the Czechoslovak nation's fight for democracy and independence, the city was crucial.

Nazi Germany seized Brno during World War II, and the Holocaust had a significant impact on the Jewish community. Brno rose to prominence as a major economic and cultural hub in the postwar Czechoslovak Socialist Republic.

Brno and the rest of Czechoslovakia underwent the transition to democracy with the fall of communism in 1989 and the Velvet Revolution that followed. Following the peaceful breakup of Czechoslovakia in 1993, it was incorporated into the newly established Czech Republic.

Brno has grown quickly in recent years and is now a dynamic city renowned for its creativity, research, and cultural activities. Its expanding reputation as a vibrant and dynamic city is largely due to the multinational firms, students, and visitors that it has drawn.

Brno's numerous architectural forms, which range from Gothic cathedrals and medieval fortifications to modernist and contemporary buildings, reflect the city's rich history. The city's ongoing preservation and celebration of its historical and cultural legacy makes it a fascinating travel destination for history buffs.

The history of Brno, which has molded the city into what it is today, is complex and fascinating, as can be seen in this summary. Visiting Brno's historical sights and landmarks enables visitors to learn more about the city's enthralling past.

## 1b. Location and Climate

**Geography**: Brno is situated in the Czech Republic's South Moravian Region in Central Europe. It is located in the southeast of the nation at the meeting point of the Svratka a Svitava rivers. The city is encircled by lovely hills and vineyards, which enhance its natural attractiveness.

Brno's topography is distinguished by a mixture of flat and steep terrain. While the surroundings around the city center are covered with forests and rolling hills, the city itself is situated in a basin. The neighboring Moravian Karst is known for its karst terrain, which includes caverns, sinkholes, and underground rivers. It is a protected natural reserve.

**Climate:** Brno experiences four different seasons in a moderate climate. The various seasons are described here along with their traits:

**Spring (March to May):** After the winter, Brno experiences a mild spring that progressively warms up. From about 5°C (41°F) in March to 20°C (68°F) in May, the temperature ranges. A fantastic time to travel is when the city starts to bloom with vibrant flowers and plants.

**Summer (June to August):** Brno experiences warm, largely sunny summers. Temperatures can occasionally rise above the average range of 20°C (68°F) to 25°C (77°F). Typically, July is the warmest month. Exploring the city's parks and gardens as well as participating in events are all very popular at this time.

**Autumn (September to November):** As the season moves along, Brno experiences pleasant temperatures that progressively drop. Temperatures in September can still be mild, hovering at 18°C (64°F), but by November, they have dropped to roughly 5°C (41°F). During this time, the city is covered in stunning fall leaves, which creates a gorgeous setting.

**Winter (December to February):** Brno experiences chilly winters with regular below-freezing temperatures. The two coldest months are December and January, with average temperatures between -2°C (28°F) and 2°C (36°F). It frequently snows, giving the area a winter wonderland feel. It's a perfect time to see the city's interior attractions and colorful marketplaces.

Brno experiences average annual precipitation, with June and July being the wettest months. When traveling, it is important to have an umbrella or raincoat with you.

A variety of options for outdoor activities, sightseeing, and taking in the area's natural beauty are provided by Brno's varied geography and changing seasons.

1c. **How to Get to Brno**

Due to its strategic location and extensive transportation infrastructure, getting to Brno is generally simple. The following are the main ways to go to Brno:

**By Air:** Brno-Turany Airport (BRQ), which is situated about 10 kilometers (6 miles) south of the city center, is the closest international airport to Brno. It offers domestic flights as well as a few foreign ones. The largest international airport in the Czech Republic, Václav Havel Airport (PRG), is another option for travelers. Brno may be reached from Prague in around 2.5 to 3 hours by train, bus, or vehicle.

**In a train:** Major cities in the Czech Republic and its neighboring countries can be reached by train from Brno. Brno's centrally positioned major train station is known as Brno hlavní nádra (Brno main station). Regular direct train service is available to Budapest,

Prague, Vienna, Bratislava, and other nearby cities. The length of the train ride depends on the final location.

**By Bus:** Regional and international bus services to and from Brno are provided by several bus companies. Near the city center is Zvonarka, a contemporary bus station. Popular bus companies FlixBus and RegioJet offer connections from Brno to numerous European locations.

**By Car:** Brno is conveniently accessible by automobile thanks to its excellent road connections. The D1 and D2 highways link Brno to Prague and Bratislava, respectively. In general, the Czech Republic's road system is well-maintained. Before driving, it's crucial to familiarize oneself with the local traffic laws and ordinances.

**Using Public Transit:** You can go to Brno using the huge domestic public transit system if you are already in the Czech Republic. From towns and cities all around the country, trains and buses run frequently. Public transit is dependable and effective in the Czech Republic.

Once in Brno, navigating the city is simple thanks to the enormous tram and bus network that the city has to offer. There are also lots of taxis available.

Before your trip, it is advisable to check timetables, purchase tickets as far in advance as you can, and take into account any travel restrictions or prerequisites, particularly during busy travel times or while going abroad.

Overall, Brno is a convenient and straightforward destination for travelers due to its accessibility by air, rail, bus, and automobile, as well as its well-connected public transportation system.

## 1d. Navigating Brno

Thanks to its well-developed public transit system and pedestrian-friendly city center, getting around Brno is quite simple and convenient. The main methods of transportation in Brno are as follows:

**Using Public Transit:**
The Brno Public Transport Company (DPMB) runs a large and effective public transportation system in the city. The entire city and its environs are serviced by trams, buses, and trolleybuses. Tickets can be bought at ticket vending machines, DPMB kiosks, or mobile apps. Single-ride tickets have a set time limit during which

they are valid, enabling transfers between various forms of transportation during that period.

**Trams:**
In Brno, trams are a well-liked method of transportation. They offer convenient and regular service in all areas of the city, including the downtown and important neighborhoods. Tram lines in Brno encompass the majority of the city's tourist sites and significant areas, making them a great method to get around.

**Buses:**
Buses are a useful adjunct to the tram network, expanding service to places the trams can't go. They provide connectivity to nearby residential areas, suburbs, and farther-off locations. For getting too specific sights or exploring places outside of the city center, buses are especially helpful.

**Trolleybuses:**

Additionally, Brno features a trolleybus system that runs on electricity provided by overhead wires. Within the city, trolleybuses offer dependable service that adheres to set routes.

**Cycling and Walking**

The city core of Brno is small and convenient for pedestrians, making it the perfect place to explore on foot. The majority of the major sights, stores, and eateries can be reached on foot. Additionally, the city boasts a well-established system of bicycle lanes that allow visitors to rent bicycles and tour the city on two wheels.

**Ridesharing and Taxis:**

In Brno, taxis are available and can be ordered through a taxi company or called on the street. In the city, there are also ride-sharing services like Uber and Bolt that provide practical transit choices.

**Renting a car:**
You may rent a car in Brno from some rental companies if you want the flexibility of driving. But bear in mind that finding parking in the city's core can be difficult, and that some places can have rules or need permits.

The majority of travelers favor using Brno's public transportation because it is dependable, reasonably priced, and simple to use. Additionally, the city's small size and pedestrian-friendly design make exploring the city center on foot fun.

# 2 ESSENTIALS TIPS

## 2a. Money and Exchange Rates:

Czech korunas (CZK) are used as money in the Czech Republic. The following are some crucial details about money and exchange rates in Brno:

**Change of Currencies:**

At banks, exchange bureaus, and a few hotels in Brno, you can exchange foreign currency for Czech koruna. Although they can have fewer hours of operation, banks often offer competitive rates. Exchange offices can be found everywhere, including at the train station, the airport, and the city center. Before engaging in any purchase, it is advised to compare exchange rates and costs.

## ATMs:

There are many ATMs (cash machines) in Brno, and they often provide a convenient means to withdraw Czech koruna. Major credit and debit cards like Visa and Mastercard are typically accepted at ATMs. It's best to verify with your bank about any foreign transaction costs since some ATMs may impose a withdrawal fee.

## Charge cards:

In Brno, hotels, restaurants, stores, and other facilities all accept credit cards, particularly Visa and Mastercard. Nevertheless, it's always a good idea to have extra cash on hand because some local vendors or smaller businesses might only accept cash payments. To prevent any problems with card usage, let your bank or credit card company know about your vacation intentions.

## Rates of currency exchange:

Exchange rates alter and are affected by several variables, including market conditions. Before your travel, it is a good idea to look up the current exchange rates to get an idea of how much the Czech koruna is worth with your home currency. Most frequently, financial websites or online currency converters offer the most recent exchange rate data.

## 2b. Communication and Language:

Czech is the nation of the Czech Republic's official language. The following information relates to language and communication in Brno:

### Russian Language:

You'll largely run into Czech speakers when in Brno. Even though many individuals, especially in touristy areas and businesses, can communicate in some English, learning a few fundamental Czech pleasantries and phrases are always welcomed. In general, locals are appreciative of attempts to communicate in their language.

**English Language Proficiency:**
In hotels and restaurants, especially among the younger generations in Brno, English is frequently spoken. The level of proficiency can vary from person to person, and some older residents might not speak English very well. It's a good idea to keep a little translation reference or a phone app on you at all times for assistance.

**Advertising and information**
Visitors can more easily navigate the city of Brno because most signs and information about the public transportation system are often presented in both Czech and English. There are frequently numerous languages,

including English, accessible for maps, brochures, and other visitor information.

**Tools and Apps for Languages**:
Language programs like Google Translate or offline translation dictionaries might be helpful for rapid translations and conversation if you desire additional language support.

Overall, even though English is widely spoken in Brno, having some basic Czech language skills and carrying translation tools might improve your interactions and communication while there.

## 2d. Regional Customs and Protocol

Knowing the customs and etiquette of the area before visiting Brno will help you have a courteous and enjoyable trip. To remember, have the following in mind:

**Greetings:**
In Brno, a handshake is the customary way to welcome someone when you first meet them. Maintaining eye contact while grinning warmly. In Czech, saying "Dobr den" (Good day) or "Dobr veer" (Good evening) is common.

**Punctuality:**
In Brno, being on time is appreciated. To be on time for scheduled meetings, appointments, or social events is considered polite. It is usual to let the other individual or group know if you expect to be late.

**Fashion Code:**

Although Brno generally has a casual dress code, it's crucial to dress correctly for particular events and locations. It's best to wear modest apparel and refrain from provocative or unpleasant attire when attending formal events, visiting churches, or other places of culture.

**Dining Manners:**

It is usual to wait until the host or the oldest person at the table starts eating when dining in restaurants or at someone's house. Keeping your hands on the table is considered courteous, however, resting your wrists on the edge of the table is not. Before beginning to eat, it's customary to say "Dobrou chu" (Enjoy your meal).

**Tipping:**

In Brno, tipping is usual. Unless a service charge is already included, it is traditional to leave a gratuity of about 10% of the entire bill in restaurants. In pubs, cafes, and for services like taxi rides, gratuities are also valued for excellent service.

**Public Conduct:**
Keep a respectful attitude at all times when in public areas. Refrain from speaking aloud or making noise. In general, smoking is not permitted in indoor public places like bars and restaurants.

Language aspects to consider
Even though English is widely spoken in tourist regions, it is nevertheless appreciated if you make an effort to learn a few fundamental Czech words and pleasantries. In Czech, saying "prosm" (please) and "dekujin" (thank you) is respectful and demonstrates respect for the community's traditions.

**Religious etiquette and cultural landmarks:**

It's crucial to observe regional customs and traditions when visiting religious or cultural places. Dress modestly, adhere to any directions or policies given, and refrain from becoming disruptive.

You may encourage positive relationships and make a good impression on the people of Brno by being aware of and respecting the local customs and etiquette. Keep in mind that adhering to local norms can improve your trip in general.

## 2e. Safety Advice

Generally speaking, it is safe to travel to Brno, but you should always be cautious and aware of your surroundings. Here are some precautions you should take while there:

## General Security

Be mindful of your possessions and keep an eye on them, especially when using public transit or in crowded areas.

Use a money belt or hold your bag close to your body to secure your possessions and keep valuables hidden from view.

Keep to populated, well-lit locations, especially at night.

Be aware of your surroundings and believe in your gut. It's best to leave a situation if something makes you feel uneasy or endangered.

## Transport Security:

Use trusted, authorized taxi services or ride-sharing applications when traveling, especially late at night.

Keep an eye on your possessions and be on the lookout for pickpockets when utilizing public transit, especially in crowded places like tram or bus stations.

If you're driving, become familiar with local traffic regulations, observe speed limits, and park in places that are well-lit and secure.

**Emergency Planning:**

Keep a copy of crucial documents in a secure location apart from the originals, including your passport, identity, and emergency contact information.

Make sure your travel insurance covers theft, accidents, and medical emergencies.

Learn where the closest hospital, embassy or consulate, and police station are located.

**Health and cleanliness:**

Consider taking essential health precautions, such as drinking plenty of water, wearing sunscreen, and washing your hands frequently.

Keep food and water safety in mind. Be cautious while eating street food or at restaurants with dubious sanitation standards, and always drink bottled water.

Local laws and ordinances

Learn the local laws and ordinances, such as those concerning drinking and driving, and any particular limitations for visiting religious or cultural sites.

## 2f. Emergency Contact Info:

Here are the crucial emergency numbers in Brno in case of an emergency:

Fire, ambulance, and emergency services: 112
158 police.

Emergency Medical Services and Ambulances: 155

150 Fire Department

Police assistance for non-emergencies: 156

It's a good idea to store these phone numbers in your phone or keep them nearby for easy access while you're in Brno. Keep your composure and provide the emergency services operator with all the information they require in case of an emergency.

Recall that having the right information, exercising caution, and taking the appropriate safety precautions can all help ensure that your trip to Brno is safe and enjoyable.

## 3  EXPLORING BRNO

## 3a. Brno City Center

The bustling downtown of Brno is home to a unique fusion of the city's past, present, and future. You can discover the following significant elements and sights in the city center of Brno:

**Freedom Square.**
Freedom Square, one of the biggest squares in Europe, is where most people congregate in Brno. Beautiful architectural landmarks like the Old Town Hall and St. Peter & Paul Cathedral surround it. The square serves as a gathering place for numerous cultural activities, dining, and shopping.

**Cathedral of Saints Peter and Paul:**
The St. Peter and Paul Cathedral, which dominates Brno's skyline, is a beautiful blend of Gothic and Baroque design. The cathedral's interiors are exquisite,

with stunning stained glass windows and a crypt that contains the remains of important personalities from Brno's past.

## Castle SPilberk:

SPilberk Castle is a well-known landmark in Brno, perched on a hilltop with a panoramic view of the city. It started as a royal fortress and has since functioned as a castle, a prison, and a museum. Discover its intriguing past, stroll along the ramparts for sweeping views of the city, and explore the exhibition spaces there.

## Ancient Town Hall

On Freedom Square, there is a historic structure called the Old Town Hall. It is a masterpiece of architecture with its distinctive tower and vibrant exterior. Inside, you may find the Brno Tourist Information Center, which offers useful tools for travelers, and take in exhibitions that highlight the city's history.

**Denis Gardens:**(Denisovy sady)

Denis Gardens, a tranquil haven in the middle of the city, provides a break from the busy streets. The park offers breathtaking views of the city, attractive pond vistas, and nicely planted gardens. It's the ideal location for a picnic or stroll.

**Brno Cemetery:**

The Brno Ossuary is an unusual and solemn attraction that can be found below the Church of St. James. It is a subterranean crypt containing the bones of about 50,000 people. This eerie location serves as a reminder of Brno's past and offers an insight into its history.

**Mendel Museum:**

Gregor Mendel, the founder of modern genetics, was born in Brno. His experiments and discoveries are shown in the Mendel Museum, which is devoted to his life and work. It is situated in the Augustinian Abbey where Mendel carried out his revolutionary genetic studies.

**Vila Tugendhat (vt):**
Vila Tugendhat, a Ludwig Mies van der Rohe architectural masterpiece, is a UNESCO World Heritage Site. Visitors can take guided tours of this famous modernist mansion to see its distinctive features and learn about its historical significance.

**Underground in Brno:**
Explore the vast network of tunnels and cellars that runs beneath the city. The Brno Underground Tour leads you through a maze of tunnels while illuminating the city's secret medieval past.

**Dining and shopping**

The city center of Brno is home to a large number of retailers, boutiques, and department stores that provide a variety of shopping alternatives. You may discover something to suit every taste, from cutting-edge clothing to regional mementos. There are several eateries, cafes, and pubs in the area where you may sample both regional and foreign cuisine.

The city core of Brno is a fascinating fusion of tradition, culture, and modernity. It provides tourists with a full and immersive experience, both in terms of its majestic landmarks and its energetic environment. Spend some time strolling the streets, taking in the atmosphere, and finding all the hidden gems.

3b. **Castle Spilberk**

The historical fortification known as Spilberk Castle is situated atop a hill in Brno, Czech Republic. What you should know about this wonderful attraction is as follows:

**History:**
The history of Spilberk Castle is lengthy and complex, dating back to the 13th century. It was initially constructed as a royal castle and used as a strategic fortress to guard the city. It served as a royal house, a military fortress, and a notorious prison, and saw numerous architectural changes over the years.

**Architecture:**
Romanesque, Gothic, Renaissance, and Baroque design aspects may all be seen in the castle's architecture. It has an imposing presence due to the towering fortifications, thick walls, and defenses. A network of

houses, courtyards, and a perfectly maintained moat may be found inside.

## Museum at Spilberk Castle:

The castle now houses the Spilberk Castle Museum, which presents information about its past as well as several exhibits. Learn more about the castle's history as a fortress, its military past, and the historical importance of Pilberk as a jail in the permanent exhibitions. The museum offers a fascinating look into the history of the castle and the people who either resided there or were held captive there.

## Tower and 360-degree Views:

You'll be rewarded for climbing the castle's tower with stunning panoramas of Brno and its surroundings. You can see the city skyline, the undulating hills, and significant sites like the Cathedral of St. Peter and Paul from this vantage point.

**Cultural events and activities:**
Concerts, exhibits, plays, and historical reenactments are just a few of the events that Spilberk Castle hosts every year. If there are any events scheduled during your visit, check the castle's calendar.

**Gardens and Castle Grounds**
Enjoy the exquisitely designed gardens and the castle grounds by taking a stroll through them. The grounds feature tranquil green areas, inviting walkways, and benches where you can unwind and take in the scenery.

**Youngsters' Museum**
A children's museum called "The Magical World of Fairy Tales" is located within the castle complex; it provides interactive exhibits and activities for younger guests, making it a joyful and instructive experience for families.

**Accessibility:**

Despite being on a hill, Spilberk Castle is reachable on foot or by public transportation. To make it simpler for visitors to go to the summit, a funicular railway connects the castle to the city center.

Spilberk Castle tours provide you with a look into Brno's past, offer breathtaking vistas, and immerse you in the architectural splendor of the castle. For lovers of history, culture, and anybody interested in learning more about the city's rich background, it's a must-see site.

**3c. Labyrinth Underground in Brno**

The enormous network of tunnels and cellars that runs beneath Brno, Czech Republic, is known as the Brno Underground Labyrinth. What you need to know about this fascinating underground attraction is as follows:

**History:**
The history of the underground labyrinth dates back to the Middle Ages. Originally, the vaults and tunnels served as both storage areas and places of safety during times of conflict. The labyrinth grew through time and developed into a sophisticated network connecting various areas of the city.

**Discovering and Tours:**
Today, guided excursions allow guests to explore a segment of the Brno Underground. These excursions lead you through a network of underground corridors that resembles a maze while showcasing the city's hidden past and secrets. The significance of the

underground areas, the activities that occurred there, and the purpose of the tunnels are all revealed by knowledgeable guides.

**Vaults and cellars:**
Merchants, craftspeople, and Brno citizens once used the tunnels and vaults that make up the underground labyrinth. These rooms served as residential quarters as well as storage and working areas. You may see the varied architectural designs and layouts of these underground chambers as you explore.

**Mysteries and Legends**
Some of the legends and mysteries surrounding the Brno Underground are revealed during the guided excursions. The history of Brno is made more fascinating by rumors of hidden wealth and secret organizations that are connected to the underground labyrinth.

**cultural gatherings and displays:**

Cultural gatherings and exhibitions are periodically held in underground rooms. These occasions include everything from theater productions and concerts to historical exhibits and art installations. If there are any events scheduled during your visit, check the schedule.

**Security and Accessibility:**

There are authorized entrance locations in the city center where you can enter the underground labyrinth. The subterranean may contain low ceilings and tight spaces, so keep in mind that people who have mobility concerns or claustrophobia may not want to spend much time there. To ensure a secure and enjoyable experience, it's crucial to heed the advice and directions of the tour guides.

You can gain a fascinating perspective on the city's history and discover its secret depths by exploring the Brno Underground Labyrinth. The underground labyrinth in Brno offers a unique and unforgettable experience, regardless of your interests in history, architecture, or simply seeking an unusual adventure.

### 3e). Petrov Hill and St. Peter and Paul Cathedral

The Cathedral of St. Peter and Paul and Petrov Hill are both notable monuments in Brno, Czech Republic. What you should know about this historic location is as follows:

**The Petrov Hill**

The important hill known as Petrov Hill, also spelled Petrov, is situated in the heart of Brno. With its elevated position above the old town, it provides sweeping views of the city and its surroundings. The historic Cathedral of St. Peter and Paul is located on the hill, which has long served as a strategic location for Brno.

**St. Peter and Paul Cathedral:**
On Petrov Hill, there is a magnificent Gothic and Baroque cathedral called the Cathedral of St. Peter and Paul. It is a city icon and one of Brno's most well-known landmarks. The cathedral's main characteristics are listed below:

The cathedral's architecture is a remarkable fusion of Gothic and Baroque design features. It is a striking sight from both the inside and the outside thanks to the twin towers, the tall arches, and the fine detailing.

**Interior:** Enter the cathedral to view the opulent interior. The opulent furnishings, stunning stained glass windows, and soaring ceilings create a tranquil and awe-inspiring ambiance. Religious sculptures and artwork adorn the main altar and side chapels.

**Crypt:** Several significant personalities from Brno's past are interred in the crypt, which is located beneath the cathedral. Visitors are welcome to tour the crypt and see where bishops, lords, and other notable people are buried.

**Bell Tower:** For a bird's-eye perspective of Brno, climb the bell tower. Although the ascent can be a little difficult, the spectacular views make the effort worthwhile.

**Observation Deck at Petrov:**

An observation platform with breathtaking vistas of Brno is located on Petrov Hill, next to the Cathedral of St. Peter and Paul. Enjoy the expansive views of the city's landmarks, rooftops, and the surrounding countryside. It's a fantastic location for taking pictures and admiring Brno's beauty from above.

**Background and Importance**:

The history of the Cathedral of St. Peter and Paul dates back to the eleventh century. Over the years, it has seen a variety of architectural transformations and historical occurrences. The cathedral is a venue for religious services, musical performances, and other cultural events and is of great religious and cultural significance to the people of Brno.

**Access:**

The Cathedral of St. Peter and Paul and Petrov Hill are both conveniently located in the heart of Brno. The hill can be climbed on foot or by using the funicular railway that runs from the mountaintop to the lower town. Visitors are welcome to the cathedral, and they can take guided tours to learn more about its significance and history.

To fully experience Brno's history, architecture, and spirituality, visit Petrov Hill and the Cathedral of St. Peter and Paul. Both tourists and residents should visit because of the breathtaking vistas and peaceful atmosphere.

3f). **Freedom Plaza**

Námst Svobody, also known as Freedom Square in Czech, is a lively public space in the center of Brno,

Czech Republic. What you should know about this famous square is as follows:

**Overview:**
One of the biggest squares in all of Europe, Freedom Square is the focal point of Brno. It serves as a center of attraction for both locals and visitors. Historical structures, shops, cafes, and cultural attractions line all four sides of the square.

**History:**
Since the 13th century, the square has had a long and rich history. It has been the site of important occasions and has been essential to Brno's growth. The square changed in several ways over time, displaying various architectural designs and urban planning strategies.

**Landmarks and interesting places:**

**St. Peter and Paul Cathedral**: At one end of Freedom Square, the towering St. Peter, and Paul Cathedral is located. Its twin towers are a recognizable symbol of the city and dominate Brno's skyline.

**Old Town Hall:** The Old Town Hall, which is a beautiful building with a recognizable tower, is situated on Freedom Square. The Brno Tourist Information Center is located within and offers useful tools for travelers.

**Parnas Fountain:** The Parnas Fountain is a well-known monument with sculptures in the middle of Freedom Square. People frequently congregate at the fountain as a gathering place.

**Festivals and Events:**
Freedom Square is a bustling location where several events, festivals, and marketplaces take place all year

long. The area is a bustling center of activity and entertainment, hosting everything from musical performances and cultural events to Christmas markets and art exhibitions.

**Dining and shopping**

A shopper's paradise, the square is flanked by businesses, boutiques, department stores, and shopping centers. There are many different shopping alternatives available, ranging from regional boutiques to global names. Freedom Square also has a ton of cafes, restaurants, and pubs where you can unwind, eat, and take in the lively ambiance.

**Using Public Transit:**

Public transportation links Freedom Square with the rest of the city are excellent. Visitors may readily access the square because it is served by numerous tram and bus routes that travel through or close to it.

**Cultural Relevance:**

For the inhabitants of Brno, Freedom Square is significant both historically and culturally. It has served as a location for protests, rallies, and events. Even the name of the square honors the city's illustrious past and links to freedom and democracy.

By going to Freedom Square, you can experience Brno's energetic environment, learn about the city's historical sites, delight in the city's shopping and dining options, and take part in the city's exciting events. It is a must-see location that perfectly encapsulates Brno's past and present.

3g). **Tugendhat Villa**

A masterpiece of architecture and a UNESCO World Heritage Site, Villa Tugendhat is situated in Brno, Czech Republic. What you should know about this famous villa is as follows:

**Architecture and history**:
Famous architect Ludwig Mies van der Rohe created Villa Tugendhat in the 1920s for the Tugendhat family. It is regarded as one of the most significant works of modernist architecture in existence. The villa exemplifies Mies van der Rohe's distinguishing style of clear lines, spacious interiors, and seamless outdoor integration.

**Design and features:**
The villa is distinguished by its creative use of materials and simple design. Some noteworthy characteristics are:

an open floor concept that makes moving between spaces easy.

large glass walls that make it difficult to tell indoors from outdoors.

the utilization of pricey materials like onyx, marble, and rare woods.

A central heating system, built-in furnishings, and a movable glass wall are among the cutting-edge technology features.

## Function and Objectives:

To give a cozy and practical living environment while presenting the most recent developments in architecture and design, Villa Tugendhat was created as a family house. At the time, it was renowned for having cutting-edge facilities like an elevator, a garage with a car lift, and servant's quarters with contemporary conveniences.

**Presented Tours:**

Today, Villa Tugendhat is accessible to the general public and offers guided tours that give information about the villa's past, present, and restoration. Visitors are given guided tours of several rooms, including the living quarters, the main hall, the garden, and the terrace, allowing them to personally feel the distinctive architectural features and spatial qualities.

**Cultural Relevance:**

In addition to its architectural worth, Villa Tugendhat is significant for its historical and cultural significance. It marks a turning point in architectural history and is an example of early 20th-century modernism. The villa's preservation and listing on the UNESCO World Heritage List emphasize how important it is to the history of architecture worldwide.

**Visitors' details:**

Access to the villa is restricted due to its fragility, thus it is advised to reserve guided visits in advance. To safeguard the ancient flooring, visitors must cover their shoes while doing the tour. The use of cameras is permitted in specific places.

A rare chance to discover Mies van der Rohe's architectural genius and take in the elegance and originality of modernist architecture is to visit Villa Tugendhat. Anyone interested in the development of architectural styles, architecture enthusiasts, or lovers of design must go there.

## 3h).Musée Mendel

In Brno, Czech Republic, there is a museum called the Mendelianum, also referred to as the Mendel Museum.

It is devoted to Gregor Mendel, a significant scientist who is regarded as the founder of modern genetics. What you need to know about this museum is as follows:

**Gregor Mendel's Scientific Discovery:**
Scientist and Augustinian priest Gregor Mendel performed ground-breaking research on pea plants in the middle of the 19th century. His work established the rules of heredity and laid the groundwork for understanding genetic inheritance. Mendel's discoveries were initially disregarded but subsequently received attention, becoming a pillar of contemporary biology.

**Museum Displays:**
The Mendel Museum has displays that highlight Mendel's life, scientific discoveries, and the era in which he lived. Mendel's experiments are covered in-depth in the museum, along with his procedures, findings, and

guiding ideas. To assist visitors to comprehend the principles of genetics, it has interactive displays, plant specimens, and replicas of Mendel's original laboratory equipment.

## The Mendel Garden

A copy of Mendel's experimental garden, where he carried out his well-known pea plant tests, is located next to the museum. Visitors can see the qualities and attributes that Mendel researched up close in the garden, which displays several pea plant kinds. It establishes a concrete link between Mendel's scientific method and the setting where he achieved his ground-breaking discoveries.

## Presentations using audio and video

To learn more about Mendel's life and scientific accomplishments, the Mendel Museum presents audiovisual presentations. To further the understanding of Mendel's experiments and their influence on the area of genetics, these presentations frequently incorporate animations, films, and narrations.

**Educational Events and Programs:**
For visitors of all ages, the museum hosts educational programs, lectures, and workshops. These programs are designed to advance knowledge of biology, genetics, and Mendel's contributions to science. The museum also holds unique occasions, such as conferences and symposiums, that are concerned with genetics and related subjects.

**Accessibility and Place:**
Near the Cathedral of St. Thomas in the heart of Brno, in the Augustinian Abbey, is where you'll find the Mendel Museum. Parking facilities are close by, and public transportation is a breeze to get to.

A fascinating excursion into the life and work of Gregor Mendel and the origins of contemporary genetics can be had by visiting the Mendel Museum. It offers a chance to recognize Mendel's scientific brilliance, the importance of his findings, and their influence on our comprehension of biological processes and inheritance. For individuals who are interested in the development of science and genetics, the museum is a must-visit location.

### 3i).Brno Zoo

Zoo Brno, sometimes referred to as the Brno Zoo, is a well-liked tourist destination in Brno, Czech Republic. Visitors can enjoy a variety of educational and recreational opportunities when visiting this place, which is home to a wide collection of animals from around the world. What you should know about Brno Zoo is as follows:

**zoological collection**
There are many different kinds of animals at the Brno Zoo, including fish, birds, reptiles, amphibians, and mammals. The zoo has an emphasis on conservation and tries to safeguard threatened animals. Lions, giraffes, elephants, zebras, penguins, crocodiles, snakes, and many other creatures can be seen in the Brno Zoo.

**Habitats and exhibits:**
The zoo has well-constructed habitats that reflect the animals' natural habitats. These habitats are skillfully built to give the animals plenty of room, enrichment, and stimulation. Visitors may get a close-up look at the creatures while learning about their habitats and typical behavior.

**Breeding initiatives and conservation initiatives:**

The Brno Zoo regularly participates in international breeding programs for threatened and endangered species, helping to protect and conserve them. The zoo interacts with other zoos and organizations across the world to promote conservation efforts and is involved in several research and conservation activities.

**Educational initiatives and programs:**

For visitors of all ages, the Brno Zoo offers educational programs and activities. These consist of narrated tours, engaging displays, live animal feedings, and instructive workshops. The zoo seeks to increase public awareness of the need to preserve natural environments, biodiversity, and wildlife.

**Child's Playground**

A designated children's section at the Brno Zoo offers fun and instructive activities for younger visitors. Playgrounds, interactive exhibits, and unique activities are all present in the region to educate kids about nature and animals.

**Infrastructure and Amenities:**

To improve the tourist experience, the zoo offers a variety of amenities. These consist of coffee shops, picnic spots, gift shops, and stroller rental services. The zoo has paved walkways and accommodations for those with impairments so that it is accessible to all visitors.

**Activities and Exhibits:**

The Brno Zoo conducts special events and exhibitions throughout the year, including themed festivals, animal displays, and holiday festivities. These occasions present exceptional chances to discover more about certain animal species, their habitats, and conservation initiatives.

**Environment-related Programs:**
The Brno Zoo is dedicated to sustainability and carries out several environmental projects. Within the zoo grounds, it encourages recycling, energy saving, and ecologically friendly behaviors.

A great opportunity to get close to nature, discover various animal species, and support conservation efforts is to go to the Brno Zoo. All ages of individuals, families, and animal lovers can enjoy and learn from this event.

3j). **Planetarium and Observatory in Brno**

The intriguing scientific and educational Brno Observatory and Planetarium is situated in Brno, Czech Republic. It gives visitors the ability to discover the wonders of the cosmos, discover astronomy, and take part in interactive activities. What you need to know about the planetarium and observatory in Brno is as follows:

**Astronomy displays:**

Several exhibits highlight the wonders of astronomy and space exploration in the observatory and planetarium. These exhibits frequently feature hands-on activities, astronomical object replicas, educational panels, and multimedia presentations. The solar system, galaxies, stars, and other astronomical phenomena are all available for study by visitors.

**Shows at planetariums:**

A giant hemisphere screen in the planetarium's domed theater displays spectacular audiovisual performances. These performances recreate the night sky, allowing viewers to travel through space and time virtually. Numerous subjects are covered in the planetarium shows, including constellations, planets, deep space objects, and cosmic processes.

**Observations concerning the sky:**

Visitors to the observatory have the chance to see astronomical objects using telescopes. Visitors can be in awe of the moon, planets, stars, and other celestial wonders during regular observation hours. Knowledgeable staff members are frequently on hand to share information and respond to inquiries regarding what you are seeing.

**Educational Workshops and Programs:**

For visitors of all ages, the Brno Observatory and Planetarium offer a variety of educational events and activities. A deeper understanding of astronomy, space science, and the natural world is the goal of these programs. They might include talks, practical exercises, and workshops devoted to certain astronomical subjects.

**Astronomical Lectures and Events:**
The organization often hosts astronomy-related special events, seminars, and presentations for the general public. At these gatherings, eminent academics, scientists, and astronomers impart their expertise and ideas on the most recent breakthroughs and developments in the field.

**Astronomical Tower:**
An observation tower with sweeping views of the surroundings is frequently part of the observatory.

Visitors can climb the tower for breathtaking views of Brno and its surroundings, making it a fantastic location for photography and taking in the natural beauty.

**Facilities and a gift shop:**
Typically, the observatory and planetarium feature a gift shop where guests can buy astronomy-related publications, telescopes, models, and trinkets. The building also offers services including restrooms and a café or snack bar.

Information on visiting and accessibility:
Visitors of all abilities may typically access the Brno Observatory and Planetarium thanks to its wheelchair-accessible and special needs-friendly facilities. For the most recent details on opening times, performances, and special events, it is advised to visit

the institution's website or get in touch with them in advance.

You can explore the wonders of the cosmos and increase your understanding of astronomy by going to the Brno Observatory and Planetarium, which offers an immersive and educational experience. Families, students, and anybody interested in the mysteries of the cosmos should visit.

3k). **Exhibition Center in Brno**

A significant exposition complex can be found in Brno, Czech Republic, and is called the Brno Exposition

Centre or BVV Trade Fairs Brno. A great variety of international trade fairs, exhibits, conferences, and cultural events are held in one of the biggest exhibition centers in Central Europe. What you need to know about the Brno Exhibition Center is as follows:

**Overview:**

A center for commerce, industry, and culture, the Brno Exhibition Center draws exhibitors and guests from all over the world. It spans a significant area and is made up of contemporary exhibition rooms, meeting spaces, outdoor exhibition areas, and supporting infrastructure.

**Exhibitions and trade shows:**

Throughout the year, the center holds a wide range of trade shows and exhibitions that focus on different industries and areas. These gatherings give companies a stage on which to present their goods, solutions, and innovations. Visitors can take in networking opportunities, see a variety of exhibits, and keep up with the most recent business trends.

**Services for conferences:**

Modern conference facilities are available at the Brno Exhibition Center for holding local, regional, national, and international conferences, congresses, seminars, and workshops. To make events successful, the center offers adaptable areas, cutting-edge audiovisual technology, and qualified support services.

**Events in the Arts and Entertainment:**

The Brno Exhibition Center also offers cultural and leisure events like concerts, festivals, art exhibitions, and sporting competitions in addition to trade shows and conferences. These occasions draw a wide range of attendees and add to Brno's thriving cultural scene.

**Outdoor Display Areas:**

Large-scale exhibitions, displays, and demonstrations can be held in the exhibition complex's roomy outdoor spaces. These spaces are used for outdoor machinery and equipment displays, auto shows, and other exhibitions that need a lot of room.

**Services and Amenities:**

To improve the tourist experience, the Brno Exhibition Center provides several facilities and services. These consist of eateries, coffee shops, information desks, cloakrooms, parking spaces, and Wi-Fi. The center works to create a welcoming and practical atmosphere for both exhibitors and visitors.

**Transportation and Accessibility:**

Both domestic and foreign visitors can easily access the exhibition facility because of its excellent connections to public transit systems. The facility often has ramps, elevators, and amenities that can accommodate people in wheelchairs, making it handicapped accessible.

**Environment and Accommodations:**
It is simple for exhibitors and visitors to locate lodging close to the Brno Exhibition Center because it is situated adjacent to many hotels. In addition, the facility is located close to eateries, retail areas, and entertainment centers, enabling guests to explore the city and its attractions while they are there.

The Brno Exhibition Center is a great place to learn about market trends, find fresh goods and services, and network with other businesspeople. The center provides a vibrant environment that encourages innovation, information sharing, and enjoyment, whether you're a professional visiting a trade show or a visitor interested in cultural events.

# 4 MUSEUM AND GALLERIES

## 4a. Museum of Moravia

The second-oldest and largest museum institution in the Czech Republic is the Moravian Museum, which is situated in Brno. It is devoted to the preservation, study, and display of the Moravian region's cultural and natural heritage. What you need to know about the Moravian Museum is as follows:

**History and Resources:**
Since its establishment in 1817, the Moravian Museum has gathered a sizable collection of artifacts, specimens, and records about the history, archaeology,

ethnography, geology, and natural sciences of the Moravian region. Archaeological finds, historical artifacts, geological samples, ethnographic items, and natural history specimens are only a few of the diverse objects included in the collections.

**Permanent Displays**:
The museum has ongoing displays that highlight Moravia's rich natural and cultural heritage. These exhibits shed light on the region's history, customs, and accomplishments. To engage visitors and enhance their awareness of Moravian culture and history, they frequently feature interactive displays, multimedia presentations, and educational panels.

**archaeological discoveries and sites:**
Throughout the Moravian region, the Moravian Museum is engaged in archaeological research and excavation projects. It has found and investigated

numerous important archaeological sites and finds, revealing information on the region's ancient history and former civilizations.

## Conservation and research

The museum is actively involved in scientific research as well as collection conservation and preservation. The Moravian Museum's experts and researchers conduct research, write scholarly articles, and cooperate with regional, national, and international organizations to enhance knowledge in a variety of subjects.

## Temporary Events and Exhibitions:

The Moravian Museum also presents temporary exhibitions that concentrate on particular subjects, artists, or historical eras in addition to its regular shows. Visitors can enjoy a dynamic and ever-changing experience at these shows, which highlight many facets of Moravian history, culture, and modern art. To engage the public, the museum also hosts events like lectures, workshops, and cultural performances.

**Educational Initiatives:**

For visitors of all ages, the Moravian Museum offers educational programs and activities, including guided tours, workshops, and interactive sessions. These initiatives seek to advance knowledge, comprehension, and enjoyment of Moravian history, science, and culture. They are frequently customized for various age and educational groups.

**Archives and libraries:**

Numerous libraries and archives are housed at the museum, supporting research and offering materials to academics, students, and the general public. These collections contain priceless documents about the history, culture, and natural sciences of the Moravian people as well as books, manuscripts, pictures, and maps.

**Facilities & Museum Stores:**
Typically, the Moravian Museum features gift stores where visitors can buy reproductions, books, trinkets, and other goods that are connected to the museum's holdings. The museum also offers amenities including cafeterias, restrooms, and places that are accessible to those with impairments.

Exploring the region's rich natural and cultural heritage is made possible by visiting the Moravian Museum. The museum offers a thorough and interesting experience whether you are interested in archaeology, history, or the natural sciences, or simply wish to become fully immersed in the local culture.

## 4b. Romani Culture Museum

The rich cultural history of the Romani people is preserved and promoted by the Museum of Romani Culture in Brno, Czech Republic. It attempts to inform the general public about the customs, history, and current problems that the Romani minority is facing. What you need to know about the Museum of Romani Culture is as follows:

**Background and Purpose:**
The mission of the Museum of Romani Culture, which was founded in 1991, is to preserve, study, and advance Romani culture. It seeks to dispel prejudice, stop discrimination, and promote tolerance and respect for the Romani people.

**Permanent Displays:**

The museum has ongoing displays that highlight the heritage, customs, and contributions of the Romani people. These exhibits frequently feature traditional attire, musical instruments, handicrafts, pictures, and personal narratives. The different cultural expressions and experiences of the Romani people are revealed via them.

**Temporary Events and Exhibitions:**

The Museum of Romani Culture also presents temporary exhibitions that concentrate on certain facets of Romani culture, history, or current issues in addition to its regular shows. These exhibits examine issues like immigration, identity, prejudice, and the accomplishments of the Romani people. To engage the public, the museum also hosts cultural events, plays, lectures, and workshops.

**Educational Initiatives:**

For schools, families, and other organizations, the museum offers educational activities. Visitors have the chance to take part in these activities to learn more about Romani culture, history, language, and traditions. They frequently consist of interactive games, workshops, storytelling sessions, and guided tours.

**Study and supporting materials:**

Research on Romani culture, history, and social issues is done and resources are gathered at the Museum of Romani Culture. To record and preserve Romani heritage, it works with academics, researchers, and locals. The study being done at the museum helps us comprehend Romani culture and its importance from a wider perspective.

**Community Outreach and Involvement:**

The museum works closely with the Romani community and tries to include Romani people and groups in its plans. To support their work and provide them with a forum to be heard, it works with Romani artists, performers, and academics. The museum also promotes understanding of the rights, difficulties, and accomplishments of the Romani minority.

**Archive and Library:**
The Library and Archive at the Museum of Romani Culture is home to a variety of books, periodicals, images, and documents about Romani social issues, history, and culture. Researchers, students, and the general public can use these resources to do additional research and study.

**Infrastructure and Amenities:**
The museum offers amenities like a lecture auditorium, a café, and a museum store. These facilities improve the

experience for visitors and offer chances for deeper immersion in Romani culture.

Learning about the rich cultural legacy and history of the Romani people is possible by visiting the Museum of Romani Culture. It offers a crucial platform for promoting awareness, dispelling prejudices, and encouraging respect and understanding. The displays, educational offerings, and community outreach projects of the museum support the acknowledgment and enjoyment of Romani culture as well as the advancement of social equality.

4c. **City Museum of Brno**

The Brno City Museum is a museum devoted to conserving and presenting the history, culture, and artwork of the city of Brno and its surroundings. It is situated in Brno, Czech Republic. The museum provides insights into Brno's rich legacy through a variety of displays, artifacts, and educational programs. What you need to know about the Brno City Museum is as follows:

## History and Resources:

Since its founding in 1869, the Brno City Museum has amassed a sizable collection of artifacts, works of art, and records about Brno's history and culture. The collections of the museum include items related to archaeology, fine art, decorative art, history, anthropology, and natural history, among other subjects.

## Permanent Displays:

The museum has ongoing displays that examine Brno's development, history, and cultural relevance. Archaeological finds, historical artifacts, works of art, pictures, and multimedia presentations are frequently on display at these exhibitions. They give a thorough history of Brno, from its prehistoric beginnings to its present-day identity.

**Unique Exhibits:**
The Brno City Museum also presents temporary and special exhibitions that concentrate on particular subjects, artists, or historical eras in addition to its regular displays. Visitors can enjoy a dynamic and ever-changing experience at these shows, which highlight many facets of Brno's art, history, and cultural life.

**Artwork collections**
A wide variety of fine art, including paintings, sculptures, graphic art, and applied art, are on display at the museum. These collections, which include works by regional and worldwide artists, cover a range of

periods and aesthetics. Visitors can explore Brno's artistic legacy and enjoy the city's many creative expressions.

**Archaeological Findings**

The Brno City Museum carries out excavation projects and archaeological studies in and around Brno. The museum's archaeology division has made important findings, including prehistoric settlements, Roman relics, and medieval artifacts, that illuminate the city's early past.

**Educational Initiatives:**

For visitors of all ages, the museum offers educational events and activities. To engage and inform the public about Brno's history, culture, and art, these programs provide guided tours, workshops, lectures, and interactive sessions. The museum also offers teachers and schools educational materials.

**Conservation and research**

The Brno City Museum actively pursues research, collection conservation, and documentation. To enhance knowledge and conserve Brno's cultural heritage, academics, researchers, and museum professionals affiliated with the museum conduct studies, produce scholarly works, and work with national and international institutions.

**Infrastructure and Amenities:**

The Brno City Museum offers facilities for visitors, including restrooms and accessibility features, as well as amenities like a museum store, a café, or a restaurant. These features improve the experience for visitors and offer chances for deeper involvement with the museum's offerings.

The history, culture, and art of Brno may all be experienced in-depth by visiting the city museum. Whether archaeology, fine arts, or local history are your things, the museum offers a priceless chance to discover and value the rich heritage of Brno and the area around it.

## 4d. Metropolitan Gallery

The Moravian Gallery is a visual arts museum with a sizable collection of paintings, sculptures, drawings, prints, and applied arts. It is situated in Brno, Czech Republic. It is one of the most well-known art museums in the country and features a wide variety of works from many eras and artistic movements. What you need to know about the Moravian Gallery is as follows:

**Background and Purpose:**

To gather, preserve, study, and display works of art from the Moravian region, the Moravian Gallery was founded in 1961. It is dedicated to stimulating cultural interchange, advancing the visual arts, and enhancing Brno's and the world's cultural landscape.

**Collections:**

The collection of the gallery includes works in the fine arts, sculpture, graphic arts, and applied arts, among other artistic disciplines. The collection features pieces by both well-known and lesser-known regional artists, showcasing a variety of artistic movements and styles from various historical eras.

**Permanent Displays:**

The Moravian Gallery presents highlights from its collection in its ongoing shows. These exhibitions are expertly organized to provide visitors with a sense of the

Moravian region's artistic past as well as the larger art world. The exhibits frequently include works by Czech and foreign artists, providing art lovers and the general public with a thorough and interesting experience.

**Temporary Displays**:
The Moravian Gallery also holds transient exhibitions that concentrate on certain artists, art movements, or thematic investigations in addition to its permanent collection. These exhibitions offer new viewpoints and expose viewers to cutting-edge artistic approaches, provocative ideas, and unique aesthetic expressions.

**Educational Initiatives**:
The gallery offers educational events and programs for a range of age groups, including tours, workshops, talks, and art classes. These initiatives seek to include visitors, enhance their comprehension of the artworks, and promote creativity and enthusiasm for the arts.

Additionally, the gallery provides educators and schools with educational materials.

**Studies and Publications:**
The Moravian Gallery actively participates in scholarly work, publishing, and research of its collection and shows. To contribute to the academic conversation and advance the comprehension and interpretation of the artworks it owns, it works with art historians, scholars, and researchers.

Special occasions and cultural activities:
In addition to its exhibitions, the gallery puts on special events, talks, conferences, and cultural programs. These gatherings frequently include guest speakers, artists' presentations, and performances, allowing for greater connection with the artworks and encouraging conversation between the public, specialists, and artists.

**Infrastructure and Amenities:**

The Moravian Gallery offers facilities for visitors, including restrooms and accessibility features, as well as amenities like a museum store, a café, or a restaurant. These features improve the visiting experience and offer chances for further enjoyment and investigation.

One has a rare chance to fully immerse themselves in the rich and varied world of visual arts by visiting the Moravian Gallery. The gallery offers a venue for appreciating, discovering, and being inspired by the artistic expressions of gifted artists, whether you are interested in classical masterpieces, contemporary art, or exploring the aesthetic legacy of the Moravian region.

4e. **Jurkovic House**

The Jurkovic House, also known as the Villa Jurkovic or Jurkovicova vila, is an important piece of Czech Republic architecture that can be seen in Brno. The house, which was created by renowned Slovak architect Duan Jurkovi, is a fine example of the Art Nouveau movement. What you need to know about the Jurkovic House is as follows:

**Building Design:**
The Jurkovic House is a superb illustration of the late 19th and early 20th-century architectural style known as Art Nouveau. The emphasis on organic shapes, colorful themes, and the seamless fusion of art and architecture are characteristics of the style. The home features finely detailed, curved, and a fusion of classic and modern components.

**History:**

The Löw-Beer family used The Jurkovic House as a residential residence, which was constructed between 1906 and 1907. The home was created by renowned architect and founder of the Art Nouveau movement Duan Jurkovi. Up to the 1920s, it was used as a private dwelling. Over the years, the ownership and use of the building changed multiple times.

**Construction Details:**
The home has several unique architectural elements. The Jurkovic House's exterior is embellished with beautiful carvings, floral motifs, and stylized balconies, among other elaborate decorative features. Large interior spaces with high ceilings, elaborate plasterwork, and exquisitely made wooden accents can be found. The house incorporates regional customs, folk architecture, and contemporary architectural ideas.

**Cultural Center and Museum:**

The Jurkovic House now functions as a museum and cultural hub. It gives guests the chance to examine the architectural masterpiece and discover more about Duan Jurkovi's life and career. The museum presents exhibits about regional architecture, design, and Art Nouveau, offering insights into the social and aesthetic background of the time.

**Events and Exhibitions:**
Throughout the year, the Jurkovic House offers many exhibitions, activities, and cultural events. These could include performances, talks, workshops, and transient exhibitions of art. The activities seek to honor Duan Jurkovi's architectural heritage while promoting modern art and design.

**Restoration and Preservation**
To maintain its original architectural elements and restore it to its former splendor, the Jurkovi House

underwent considerable restoration work. The building's authenticity was to be preserved, and the craftsmanship and creative vision of Duan Jurkovi were to be displayed.

**Surroundings:**

The Jurkovic House is located in a charming area of Brno that is bordered by other old homes and greenery. Visitors can enjoy the architectural attractiveness and cultural heritage of the neighborhood by taking a stroll through it.

The Jurkovic House offers a look into the realm of Art Nouveau architecture and Duan Jurkovi's vision. This architectural marvel's complex detailing, creative craftsmanship, and distinctive fusion of traditional and modern elements may all be appreciated by visitors. Through exhibitions and programs that honor art, design, and cultural history, the museum and cultural center situated within the villa provide engaging experiences.

# 5 PARKS AND GARDEN

## 5a. Luzanky Park

Large urban park Luzanky Park in Brno, Czech Republic, provides a tranquil escape from the busy city core. Luzanky Park is a well-liked location for both locals and tourists because of its lovely green areas, elegant walks, and many recreational services. What you need to know about Luzanky Park is as follows:

**History:**

The history of Luzanky Park dates back to the late 18th century. It was initially intended as an English-style landscaped garden, with ideals from the Enlightenment as influences. The park experienced numerous alterations and additions over time, becoming the stunning and varied park it is today.

**Park Features**

The huge area of Luzanky Park offers plenty of room for leisurely pursuits, recreation, and relaxation. The park's mixture of open lawns, and avenues bordered with trees, flowerbeds, and ponds creates a tranquil and lovely atmosphere. Additionally, there are lots of benches and picnic places where tourists may relax and take in the scenery.

**Recreation and Sports**

The park provides visitors with a variety of sporting and leisure opportunities. These consist of football fields, basketball courts, volleyball courts, and tennis courts. Visitors can participate in competitive games or just have fun playing with their friends and family. In addition, there are trails for jogging and cycling, offering chances for outdoor fitness activities.

**Playgrounds for kids:**
Luzanky Park offers many playgrounds to accommodate families with young children. These playgrounds contain swings, slides, climbing frames, and other playthings, guaranteeing that kids may enjoy themselves safely in the park.

**Areas for Repose**
Luzanky Park provides dedicated areas where guests can unwind and take in the natural beauty of the surroundings for those seeking peace and relaxation. These spaces frequently offer benches, shaded areas,

and quiet areas where people may relax and read a book, have a picnic, or just enjoy the quiet.

## Various Cultural Attractions

Many cultural attractions at Luzanky Park are worth visiting. The Luzanky Summer Pavilion, a masterpiece of Art Nouveau architecture that hosts a variety of cultural events, concerts, and exhibitions, is one standout feature. The park occasionally presents shows and concerts outside, enhancing its cultural value.

## Animals and Plants:

A wide variety of plant species, including mature trees, vibrant flowers, and well-kept bushes, can be found in Luzanky Park. The park is a paradise for birdwatchers and nature lovers due to the numerous bird species that are drawn there by the natural beauty of the area. Visitors can take strolls while seeing the park's wildlife and beauty.

**Amenities:**
For the comfort and convenience of tourists, Luzanky Park offers practical amenities. These consist of restrooms open to the public, water fountains, and surrounding cafes or kiosks where guests can buy drinks or snacks.

In the middle of Brno, Luzanky Park offers a tranquil and revitalizing retreat. This park offers the perfect backdrop for leisure activities, a tranquil area to unwind, or a place to admire nature. For a wonderful experience, take a stroll, play some sports, or just relax in Luzanky Park's serene setting.

5b. **Gardens, Denis**

Denis Gardens, a delightful public park in Brno, Czech Republic, is well-known for its luxuriant vegetation, serene atmosphere, and stunning views of the city. The gardens, which are perched on a hillside, provide a peaceful respite from the activity of the city. What you need to know about Denis Gardens is as follows:

**History:**

In honor of Vincenc Ferdinand Denis, a Czech publisher, and author, Denis Gardens, also known as Denisovy in Czech, was built in the 19th century. The gardens, which were originally intended as a pleasant space for the neighborhood adjacent, have since evolved into a cherished public park.

**Garden Accents:**

The gardens stand out for their well-kept lawns, manicured pathways, and an assortment of trees, shrubs, and flowers. You'll come across vibrant flower beds, attractive gazebos, and inviting seating places as you stroll through the park, where you can unwind and take in the quiet.

## 360-degree views

The amazing panoramic vistas that Denis Gardens has to offer are one of its key draws. Visitors can take in expansive views of the city of Brno, including its famous landmarks, historic structures, and scenic landscape, as the gardens are perched on a hill. Bring your camera if you want to record the breathtaking scenery.

**Art installations and sculptures:**

The park's creative component is enhanced by the numerous sculptures and artworks throughout Denis Gardens. These works of art, which range from traditional statues to modern pieces, improve the gardens' aesthetic appeal and provide visitors with places of interest.

**Relaxation and walking:**
The grounds offer the ideal location for strolls, picnics, or just finding a quiet place to unwind. It is simple to explore the gardens and take a stroll amidst the natural beauty thanks to the well-paved trails. You can relax with a book in a shady place beneath a tree or have a picnic with friends and family there.

**Activities and Shows:**
Open-air concerts, theatrical productions, and cultural festivals are just a few of the activities and performances that occasionally take place in Denis Gardens. These activities give the park life and amusement, drawing both locals and tourists.

**Nearby landmarks**
Other well-known sights in Brno are located not far from Denis Gardens. The Spilberk Castle, Brno

Observatory and Planetarium, and the Cathedral of St. Peter and Paul are just a few of the surrounding attractions that visitors may readily explore on foot.

**Amenities and Accessibility:**
With adjacent tram and bus stops, it's simple to use public transportation to get to the gardens. To enhance visitors' comfort and convenience, amenities including benches, public restrooms, and drinking fountains are placed all across the park.

In the middle of Brno, Denis Gardens provides a peaceful and attractive retreat. The gardens offer a serene sanctuary in the city, whether you're trying to take in the surrounding natural beauty, marvel at the expansive vistas, or just find a quiet place to unwind. Denis Gardens offers several opportunities for relaxation, including strolls, picnics, and taking in breathtaking views.

## 5c. Reservoir in Brno

The Brno Reservoir, sometimes referred to as the Brno Dam or Brno Lake, is a sizable reservoir that is situated in the Czech city of Brno. With a variety of activities and attractions, this man-made lake is a well-liked entertainment spot for both locals and visitors. What you need to know about the Brno Reservoir is as follows:

**Overview of a reservoir**
The Svratka River was dammed to create the Brno Reservoir. It has a maximum depth of about 38 meters and a surface area of about 260 hectares. The reservoir is surrounded by beautiful scenery, including hills,

vineyards, and forests, making for an idyllic environment for outdoor activities.

**Activities for Recreation:**
There are several chances for different recreational activities at the Brno Reservoir. The calm waters of the reservoir are perfect for swimming, sailing, windsurfing, paddleboarding, and fishing. Boat rentals are offered for people who want to explore the reservoir from the water on the lake, which is also excellent for boating. Additionally, there are beaches with designated swimming areas where guests may unwind, sunbathe, and take in the sandy shorelines.

**hiking and bicycling:**
The reservoir region is a popular spot for outdoor enthusiasts because it is bordered by lovely hiking and biking trails. By cycling or hiking through the forests and along the shores of the reservoir, visitors can

discover the picturesque surroundings. The pathways allow tourists to exercise while connecting with nature since they provide breathtaking views of the lake.

**Areas for Parks and Picnics**:
Around the Brno Reservoir, there are a lot of parks and picnic sites that offer places for leisure and family get-togethers. These places frequently have green areas, seats, and picnic tables so that people can have a picnic or BBQ while being surrounded by nature. Some parks even offer kid-friendly playgrounds, guaranteeing a good day for the whole family.

**Cafes and restaurants:**
You may find a variety of eateries, cafés, and refreshment stands along the Brno Reservoir's beaches. These places serve a variety of foods and drinks, enabling customers to grab something to eat or unwind

with a drink while admiring the picturesque views of the reservoir.

**Festivals and Events:**

Throughout the year, festivals and activities are held at the Brno Reservoir. Competitions in water sports, music festivals, cultural events, and fireworks displays may all fall under this category. These gatherings draw both locals and visitors, enhancing the reservoir area's dynamic vibe.

**Environment and Wildlife**

Many different types of plants and animals can be found in the Brno Reservoir. Many different bird species, including ducks, swans, and herons, can be seen by birdwatchers, especially in the reservoir's more tranquil regions. There are additional options for exploring and observing nature in the nearby forests and green spaces.

**Transportation and Accessibility:**

With connections from the city center to the Brno Reservoir provided by buses and trams, public transportation is simple to use. For those who prefer to arrive at the reservoir by car, there are parking sites as well.

The Brno Reservoir provides the ideal fusion of outdoor pursuits, scenic beauty, and leisure. The reservoir offers a welcome respite from the bustle of the city, whether you want to enjoy water sports, hike or bike along gorgeous pathways, or just relax by the shores. The Brno Reservoir is a well-liked location for those who appreciate the outdoors and natural beauty because of its wealth of recreational options and gorgeous vistas.

## 5d. Park at Kravi Hora Observatory

The intriguing scientific and educational Kravi Hora Observatory Park near Brno, Czech Republic, gives visitors a rare chance to investigate the mysteries of the cosmos. The observatory park, located on Kravi Hora Hill, offers breathtaking views of the city and is home to a cutting-edge observatory as well as some interactive displays. What you need to know about Kravi Hora Observatory Park is as follows:

**Overview of the Observatory**:
Modern astronomy equipment can be found at the Kravi Hora Observatory, which houses cutting-edge telescopes and equipment. It serves as a hub for astronomical observation, study, and research. The observatory's major goal is to give visitors an immersive astronomy experience and awaken a greater awareness of the cosmos.

**Astronomy displays:**

A variety of interactive exhibits and displays that study various facets of astronomy and space science are available at the observatory park. Through educational panels, models, and multimedia displays, visitors can gain knowledge about the solar system, galaxies, stars, and other astronomical phenomena. Visitors of all ages will be entertained and educated by the exhibitions.

**Planetarium:**

A planetarium is located in the Kravi Hora Observatory Park, where guests can experience virtual space voyages. Visitors to the planetarium can explore far-off galaxies, take in cosmic happenings, and learn more about our place in the universe through engaging shows that mimic the night sky. Both educational and uplifting, the immersive planetarium experience is wonderful.

**Sessions for Observation:**

Regular viewing sessions are held at the observatory, allowing guests to view celestial objects using large telescopes. Visitors may have the chance to see planets, stars, galaxies, and other intriguing phenomena depending on the weather and astronomical occurrences. There are knowledgeable staff members on hand to help tourists and to explain what they are seeing.

Events and Workshops in Astronomy:

Throughout the year, Kravi Hora Observatory Park hosts a range of astronomy-related activities, workshops, and lectures. These gatherings offer chances to explore further into particular subjects, take part in practical activities, and interact with subject-matter experts. They are geared toward different interests and age groups. For those who are interested in astronomy, these activities offer an immersive and instructive experience.

**Location and Views from a Hill:**
The observatory park, which is located atop Kravi Hora Hill, provides sweeping views over Brno and its surroundings. While strolling in the park or during observation sessions, visitors can take in the breathtaking views. The hilltop site offers a peaceful and beautiful environment for learning and observation.

**Educational Initiatives:**
The observatory park provides organized groups and schools with educational programs. Through engaging activities, narrated excursions, and specially crafted teaching material, these programs hope to introduce students and participants to the exciting world of astronomy. The shows aim to pique interest and cultivate a passion for science.

**Amenities and Accessibility:**

Bus connections from the city center make it simple to use public transportation to go to Kravi Hora Observatory Park. A parking lot, a café, and restrooms are among the park's practical features.

Anyone interested in astronomy and space science will find Kravi Hora Observatory Park to be both an entertaining and educational experience. The observatory park offers an interesting and educational trip into space, whether you're an experienced astronomer, a curious student, or simply interested in the mysteries of the cosmos. For astronomy aficionados and those looking to further their understanding of the cosmos, Kravi Hora Observatory Park is a must-visit location. It offers interactive displays, planetarium performances, observing sessions, and educational events.

# 6 DINING AND CUISINE

## 6a. Customary Czech Food

The robust, savory dishes that make up traditional Czech cuisine are renowned for reflecting the nation's extensive culinary history. Czech cuisine offers a variety of meals that are sure to satiate your taste buds. Its food is influenced by its Central European location and historical influences. You should try the following typical Czech dishes:

**Svková:** Svková is a traditional Czech cuisine that consists of beef sirloin that has been marinated and is served with a creamy vegetable sauce. Knedliky, which are bread- or potato-dough dumplings topped with cranberry sauce and a lemon slice, are frequently served with it.

Czech goulash is a robust stew made with soft beef or pork that is cooked in a thick and savory sauce composed of onions, paprika, and caraway seeds. It frequently comes with potato pancakes or bread dumplings.

**Vepo-knedlo-zelo:** Sauerkraut and dumplings are served with roasted pork in this dish. With bread or potato dumplings and sauerkraut, which gives the meal a sour and salty component, the pork is typically spiced and slow-cooked to obtain a soft texture.

**Bramboráky:** Bramboráky are typical potato pancakes from the Czech Republic. To make them, raw potatoes are grated, combined with eggs, flour, and a variety of herbs and spices, and then fried till golden brown. Sour cream or garlic sauce is frequently served with bramboráky.

Deep-fried cheese is the main ingredient of the popular Czech street dish known as "smaen sr." A slice of Edam or Hermelin cheese is typically breaded and fried till crisp and golden. It frequently comes with French fries or a side of salad and tartar sauce.

**Trdelnik:** A sweet pastry that has become popular among tourists is called . A cylindrical spit is used to roll the dough, which is then grilled until golden and crispy before being dusted with sugar and cinnamon. Trdelnk is frequently eaten as a dessert or as a street snack.

**Palainky:** Palainky is crepe-like, thin Czech pancakes. They can be filled with a variety of savory or sweet ingredients, such as cheese, fruit, chocolate, or jam. Although palacinky are typically eaten as a dessert, they can also be had for breakfast or as a snack.

Despite not being a food, Czech beer is an essential component of the nation's culinary tradition. You shouldn't pass up the chance to sample some of the well-known Czech beers, like Pilsner Urquell or Budweiser Budvar, as the Czech Republic is known for its beer production.

These are only a few of the mouthwatering dishes you can sample when learning about traditional Czech cuisine. Enjoy the hearty portions and rich flavors that make Czech cuisine so satisfying, and don't forget to pair your meal with a cold Czech beer.

## 6b. Local Cuisine in Brno:

As a bustling city with its culinary traditions, Brno offers a variety of regional dishes that are interesting to try. You should try the following regional dishes from Brno:

**Chlebicky**: Popular in Brno, are open-faced sandwiches. These bite-sized snacks are made with a variety of toppings that are artfully arranged on a slice of bread, including ham, cheese, eggs, pickles, and mayonnaise. They are ideal for a tasty, quick snack.

The dish known as **Moravian Sparrow** (Moravsk vrabec) is a specialty of the Moravian region, which includes Brno. Typically made from the shoulder or neck, it consists of roasted pork served with bread or potato dumplings, sauerkraut, and a thick gravy. A filling and flavorful dish that highlights the area's culinary heritage is Moravian Sparrow.

**Livance:** Livance are sweet pancakes resembling German or Austrian pancakes. These are often served with powdered sugar, fruit preserves, or a dollop of sour cream and are created from a yeast-based batter. Livance is frequently eaten as a sweet treat or as a dessert.

In Brno, one may find the typical Czech pastry known as "vetrnik." It is a choux pastry with vanilla cream filling and caramel frosting on top. The cream and caramel combine with the flaky, airy pastry to make a delightfully delicious dessert.

## 6c. Recommendations for Cafes and Restaurants:

There are several dining options in Brno, including cafés and restaurants serving a variety of cuisines. Here are some suggestions for restaurants where you can have a special dining experience:

The well-known restaurant **Pavillon**, which is situated in the center of Brno, is recognized for its contemporary interpretation of Czech food. It provides a fine dining experience with an emphasis on using seasonal, nearby ingredients to make unique and delectable dishes.

**Koishi:** If you're in the mood for Japanese cuisine, Koishi is a highly acclaimed restaurant in Brno. It serves real Japanese foods, including sushi, sashimi, ramen, and more. The restaurant's exquisite ambiance and competent cooks ensure an exceptional dining experience.

**Sklizeno Food Market**: Sklizeno is a unique food market idea that offers a selection of high-quality and organic items. It contains a café where you can have a freshly produced cup of coffee, as well as a range of sandwiches, salads, and other delightful delights made with locally sourced products.

**Barcelonetta**: If you're wanting Mediterranean flavors, Barcelonetta is a beautiful restaurant that provides Spanish and Catalan food. From tapas and paella to Spanish wines and sangria, Barceloneta offers a taste of the Mediterranean in the heart of Brno.

**Café Podnebí**: For a cozy and relaxing ambiance, Café Podnebí is a popular choice. This café serves a range of coffees, teas, handcrafted cakes, and light meals. It's a terrific location to unwind and take a leisurely break during your exploration of Brno.

These are only a few choices, and there are many more fantastic restaurants and cafes to discover in Brno. Whether you're in the mood for Czech cuisine, cosmopolitan cuisines, or a pleasant café experience, Brno has something to satisfy every pallet.

# 7  SHOPPING IN BRNO

### 7a. Shopping Streets and Districts

When it comes to shopping in Brno, there are various avenues and districts noted for their different retail choices. Whether you're looking for fashion, souvenirs, local products, or worldwide brands, here are some popular shopping streets and districts to explore:

Freedom Square is located at Namesti Svobody. Náměstí Svobody is the major square in Brno and a lively hive of activity. It is flanked by shops, department stores, and boutiques selling a mix of local and international brands. You may buy apparel, accessories, cosmetics, gadgets, and more in this colorful sector.

**Czech Street**
A historic pedestrian thoroughfare dotted with stores and cafes is known as the Eská thoroughfare. It has a quaint ambiance with a variety of boutiques, antique stores, bookstores, and art galleries. It's a wonderful area to explore and discover unusual things.

**The Vankovka Gallery**

Vankovka Gallery is a cutting-edge shopping complex that is close to the main train station and has a wide selection of stores, including apparel, accessories, home goods, and technology. It is a one-stop shop for shopping and amusement because it also has a food court and a movie theater.

### The Vankovka Galerie

Another well-known shopping center in Brno is Galerie Vankovka, which houses a variety of shops selling anything from electronics and home goods to clothing and beauty products. There are many options for all of your shopping needs in this roomy, contemporary shopping location.

### Palác Brnênská

A shopping center called Palác Brnênská is situated in the city of Brno, close to the major train station. It has a wide variety of stores, including supermarkets, electronics stores, and clothing outlets. The building also houses a range of eateries and coffee shops.

**Spielberk Office Building**:
Close to the city center is the Spielberk Office Centre, a contemporary complex that blends office space with retail establishments. It has a variety of stores, including apparel, household goods, and specialty shops. The complex also offers a variety of food alternatives.

**shopping center Futurum**
A sizable shopping center outside of Brno called Futurum Shopping Center is reachable via public transportation. There are several stores there, selling everything from electronics and sporting goods to clothing and accessories. In addition, the mall offers a movie theater and entertainment alternatives.

## Regional Markets

There are various local markets in Brno where you may buy seasonal vegetables, regional specialties, and one-of-a-kind handmade goods. For their lively ambiance and an extensive assortment of items, the Lidická Market and the Zeln' trh (Vegetable Market) are worth visiting.

These are only a few instances of the Brno retail areas and streets. Brno offers a diversified shopping experience where you can discover anything from local goods to international brands, whether you like contemporary retail malls, pedestrian walkways, or local markets.

7b. **Markets and Shopping Centers Popular**

There are many well-known marketplaces and shopping areas in Brno where you may buy a wide variety of goods and have a distinctive shopping experience. The following list includes some of the city's most well-known marketplaces and shopping areas:

Vegetable Market, **Zelny trh:**
Zelny trh, a historic market square that has been in use since the 13th century, is situated in the center of Brno. Fresh fruits, veggies, flowers, and herbs may all be found at this bustling market. Additionally, the market has stands offering regional goods including cheese, honey, pastries, and classic Moravian wines.

**(Lidická Market) Lidická Trznice:**
A bustling market called Lidická Trznice is located not far from the city center. Fresh fruit, meats, dairy items, baked goods, and spices are just a few of the many products it provides. The market also often hosts events like farmers' markets and craft fairs where you may find distinctive regional goods.

**Shopping Center Olympia**

One of the biggest shopping centers in Brno is Olympia Shopping Center. It contains a variety of stores, including ones for clothing, electronics, household goods, and cosmetics. The mall offers a complete shopping and leisure experience by way of a food court, restaurants, a movie theater, and entertainment facilities.

**Avion Retail Park**

Another well-known shopping area in Brno is Avion Shopping Park. It provides a variety of domestic and foreign brands, including clothing stores, shoe stores, electronics stores, and outlets for household items. Additionally, the shopping center offers a variety of restaurants and plenty of parking.

**shopping center Futurum**

On the outskirts of Brno, there is a sizable mall called Futurum Shopping Center. There are many different types of stores there, including ones for clothing, accessories, electronics, and athletic goods. The mall is a handy location for both shopping and entertainment because it also has a food court, restaurants, a movie theater, and entertainment options.

## Exhibition Vankovka:

Near Brno's main train station is the contemporary shopping center Galerie Vankovka. There are several businesses there, selling anything from clothing and cosmetics to electronics and furniture. The mall offers a complete shopping and entertainment experience with its food court, eateries, and movie theater.

## Central Market Hall, Hala C:

The Central Market Hall, usually referred to as Hala C, was recently restored in Brno. Vendors providing fresh vegetables, meats, cheeses, baked goods, and other regional goods provide a distinctive shopping experience. A few food vendors are located in the market hall where you may grab a quick snack.

Fresh vegetables and regional delicacies are available for purchase in these markets and shopping malls in Brno, as well as clothing, gadgets, and entertainment. Whether you're seeking standard household items or one-of-a-kind keepsakes, you're sure to find what you need while taking in the lively ambiance of these well-liked shopping areas.

# 8 NIGHTLIFE AND ENTERTAINMENT

## 8a. **Pubs and Bars**

Brno boasts a thriving nightlife scene with a variety of bars and pubs to accommodate different tastes and preferences. Everyone may find something in Brno, whether they're seeking a comfortable pub, a hip cocktail bar, or a buzzing beer garden. Here are a few of the city's well-liked bars and pubs:

Super Panda Circus is a distinctive bar that serves a variety of cocktails, specialty beers, and non-alcoholic beverages. It is well-known for its eccentric and artistic ambiance. The bar is a favored hangout for both locals and tourists since it frequently holds live music events, DJ performances, and art exhibitions.

**Bar, ktery neexistuje**: This secretive speakeasy-style bar, which translates to "The Bar That Does Not Exist," is a hidden gem. Inside, you'll discover a warm and welcoming setting with a focus on premium cocktails. The mixologists working at the bar can make custom drinks based on your tastes.

**Pegas:** Known for its long brewing legacy, Pegas is a historic beer hall in the city's core. The renowned Pegas lager is one of the several Czech beers available on tap at the bar. Pegas is a nice spot to gather with friends and drink a pint of beer because of its cozy ambiance and historic decor.

**Bar Naproti:** Located in the center of Brno, Bar Naproti is a hip and well-liked hangout for both residents and tourists. In a contemporary and fashionable setting, it provides a large selection of beers, both domestically and internationally. Regular events held at the bar include beer tastings and live music performances.

Klub Fléda is a well-known music bar and club where live music performances, DJ sets, and other cultural events take place. It is a popular choice for enjoying a drink while taking in the local music scene because of its welcoming and laid-back atmosphere.

**Ktery :** This secluded, cozy bar is renowned for its inventive, artistic cocktails. The menu is constantly changing, providing a distinctive drinking experience with creative flavor pairings and presentations. The difficulty in locating the entrance only adds to the allure of this hidden treasure.

U Dvou Koek is a traditional pub in the Czech Republic with a relaxed ambiance. Traditional pub fare and a selection of Czech beers are offered. Live music performances are frequently held at the pub, which fosters a fun and lively atmosphere.

L'Imperatore Bar is a chic cocktail bar with an emphasis on superior mixology. The bartenders are skilled in making both traditional cocktails and their original concoctions. The bar is a fantastic option for a chic night out thanks to its elegant ambiance and attentive service.

The bars and pubs in Brno come in a variety of styles. The city has a variety of places where you may have a drink and take in the vibrant atmosphere of the nightlife, from historic pubs to contemporary cocktail bars.

**8b. Clubs and Nightclubs:**

Brno has a vibrant nightlife scene, and if you're looking for clubs and nightclubs to dance the night away, you're in luck. Here are some popular clubs and nightclubs in Brno:

**Fleda**: Fleda is a renowned music club that hosts live concerts, DJ nights, and various cultural events. It features a spacious dance floor and multiple bars, offering a mix of music genres, including rock, electronic, indie, and more.

**Fléda Music Club**: Fléda Music Club is another popular venue for live music performances and club nights. It hosts both local and international bands and DJs, playing a wide range of music styles, from alternative and rock to electronic and dance.

**Club Faval**: Club Faval is a lively nightclub known for its energetic atmosphere and diverse music genres. It features multiple dance floors, each with its music style, including house, techno, R&B, and hip-hop. The club often hosts themed parties and events, attracting a young and energetic crowd.

**Metro Music Bar**: Metro Music Bar is a prominent nightclub located in the city center. It hosts DJ evenings, themed events, and sometimes live music performances. The club has many levels, each having a different environment and music style, catering to various tastes.

**Charlie's Hat**: Charlie's Hat is a bustling pub and nightclub that offers a range of music genres, including pop, rock, disco, and more. It boasts a retro-themed décor, bringing a nostalgic touch to the partying experience. Charlie's Hat also hosts karaoke nights and special events throughout the year.

These are only a few examples of the clubs and nightclubs in Brno. The city's nightlife culture is lively, with new locations continuously developing. It's always a good idea to check local listings and ask locals for the newest hotspots and activities happening during your visit.

## 8c. Theaters and Concert Halls:

Brno is known for its strong cultural scene, and you may enjoy a range of theater plays and concerts throughout your visit. Here are some significant theaters and concert halls in Brno:

**National Theatre Brno**: The National Theatre Brno is a historic theater that displays a wide spectrum of opera, ballet, and drama acts. The theater's magnificent architecture and excellent plays make it a must-visit for theater fans.

**Mahen Theatre:** Mahen Theatre is a stunning neoclassical theater and a component of the National Theatre Brno. It is noted for its broad repertoire of opera, theater, and ballet productions. The theater also holds international festivals and highlights creative and modern productions.

**Janáček Theatre:** Janáček Theatre is another notable theater in Brno, recognized for its modern architecture and world-class performances. The Brno National Theatre Opera performs a variety of opera and ballet productions there.

Sono Centrum is a flexible location that hosts a range of cultural events, such as concerts, theater productions, dance performances, and exhibitions. It draws both domestic and foreign artists with its intimate and contemporary environment.

VIDA! VIDA! Despite not being a standard theater, the Science Center is noteworthy for its hands-on science exhibits and performances. Visitors can discover science and technology through interactive exhibits and presentations, making it a distinctive experience.

Just a few of the theaters and concert halls in Brno are shown below. The city's cultural environment is dynamic and diverse, with several venues offering shows and events all year long. When visiting Brno, look up the most recent schedule in the local listings and take advantage of the city's diverse cultural attractions.

# 9  DAY TRIP TO BRNO

## 9a. The Cultural Landscape of Lednice-Valtice:

In the South Moravian Region, close to Brno, there is a
UNESCO World Heritage Site called the Lednice-Valtice
Cultural Landscape. It is an amazing region recognized
for its outstanding architecture, sizable parklands, and
breathtaking natural beauty. The Lednice-Valtice
Cultural Landscape Overview is as follows:

**Lednice Castle**: The epicenter of the cultural
environment, Lednice Castle is a beautiful neo-Gothic
building. It has beautiful architecture and tasteful
furnishings, including a tower that is reminiscent of a
minaret. A lovely park with lakes, bridges, and
enchanting pavilions surrounds the castle.

Another noteworthy architectural treasure in the cultural landscape is Valtice Castle. It is a baroque-style castle that once served as the home of the Liechtenstein family in power. The castle is home to a wine museum and has exquisitely planted gardens and vineyards.

The Minaret is one of the most recognizable structures in the Lednice-Valtice Cultural Landscape. This tower in Lednice Castle Park is imposing and features an Islamic design. It provides sweeping views of the neighborhood. In the Czech Republic, it is a startling and unexpected sight.

**Park and Garden Complex:** The 200 square kilometer park and garden complex is a highlight of the cultural landscape. The scenery includes lakes, ponds, tree-lined streets, and well-landscaped gardens. The park is ideal for relaxing boat trips, bicycle rides, or strolls.

**Vineyards on its borders**: The Lednice-Valtice Cultural Landscape is renowned for its wineries. Visitors can tour vineyards, sample regional wines, and learn about the wine-making process in this area, which is known for producing high-quality wines.

A network of clearly marked bike lanes and walking trails is available across the cultural landscape, allowing visitors to explore the area at their speed. It's a fantastic chance to fully experience the area's natural splendor while also finding secret treasures along the route.

**Events and Festivals:** The Lednice-Valtice Cultural Landscape holds several events and festivals every year. These allow guests to enjoy the rich local culture through music performances, wine festivals, garden exhibitions, and cultural acts.

Lednice-Valtice Cultural Landscape visits are like entering a storybook. It provides a singular and immersive experience for nature lovers, history buffs, and lovers of architecture equally with its gorgeous castles, lovely gardens, and tranquil lakes.

## 9b. Mikulov:

In the South Moravian Region of the Czech Republic, close to the Austrian border, sits the lovely town of Mikulov. It is renowned for its beautiful scenery, wineries, and old-world architecture. An overview of Mikulov is given below:

**Mikulov Castle**: Mikulov Castle, a magnificent Baroque-style building built on a hill overlooking the town, is the focal point of the community. The castle has stunning architecture, including a tower with sweeping views of the area nearby. Visitors are welcome to see the castle's interior and stop by the museum.

**Holy Hill** (Svat kopeek) is a sacred place of worship outside of Mikulov. There is a Calvary complex there with chapels and statues, as well as the Church of St. Sebastian. The hill provides a tranquil setting in addition to breathtaking views of the town and the nearby vineyards.

**Mikulov Wine Region**: The town of Mikulov is located in a well-known wine region, and winemaking is an important aspect of its history and culture. Visitors can partake in wine tastings, tour nearby wineries, and see how wine is produced. You can try a range of regional wines during the town's Mikulov Wine Festival.

**Jewish Quarter and Synagogue:** Mikulov boasts a well-maintained Jewish Quarter that highlights the town's extensive Jewish history. Visitors can see the historic synagogue, which currently houses a Jewish culture and history display, and the Jewish cemetery, which was established in the sixteenth century.

**Town Square (Námst):** The attractive Mikulov town square is bordered by vibrant Baroque and Renaissance structures. It is a bustling neighborhood with cafes, restaurants, and independent stores. The town hall and a Marian Column, a notable landmark, are also located on the square.

Mikulov is a component of the Valtice-Mikulov Landscape Area, a natural preserve distinguished by vineyards, undulating hills, and picturesque villages. The environment provides fantastic chances for outdoor pursuits like hiking, cycling, and wine tours.

A great vacation spot, Mikulov mixes history, culture, and scenic beauty. Mikulov offers a distinctive and unforgettable experience, whether you're touring its historical landmarks, indulging in wine tastings, or just taking in the peaceful ambiance.

## 9c. Brno Tugendhat Villa:

A masterpiece of modernist architecture can be found in Brno, Czech Republic, called the Tugendhat Villa. It is regarded as one of the most notable examples of functionalist architecture in the entire globe and was created by architect Ludwig Mies van der Rohe. An overview of the Tugendhat Villa is provided below:

**Architecture:** The Tugendhat Villa is noted for its avant-garde style and creative material selection. It emphasizes simplicity and functionality with an open floor plan, big glass walls, and clean lines. The line separating interior and outdoor spaces is blurred by the villa's seamless integration with the surrounding garden.

The villa was constructed for the Tugendhat family in the late 1920s and served as their primary residence. It has witnessed important historical occurrences and even served as the German headquarters during World War II. In 2012, it was reopened to the public following renovation.

The Tugendhat Villa was designated a UNESCO World Heritage Site in 2001 in recognition of its remarkable architectural significance and contribution to the growth of modern architecture.

**Guided Tours**: Visitors can take guided tours of the Tugendhat Villa to explore the interiors and discover more about its architectural significance. Due to the high demand, it is advised to make your tour reservations in advance.

Preservation and repair: To return the villa to its former glory, substantial restoration was performed. The goal of the restoration work was to reconstruct the villa as faithfully to its original design as possible, down to the distinctive onyx wall and the cutting-edge heating and ventilation systems.

Lectures, exhibits, concerts, and other cultural activities are periodically held in the Tugendhat Villa. These occasions offer additional chances to recognize the architectural and cultural significance of the mansion.

Anyone interested in modernist architecture and design must visit the Tugendhat Villa. Architects and designers all around the world are continually motivated by its classic elegance and ground-breaking ideas.

## 9d. Moravian Karst

A stunning karst terrain known as the Moravian Karst may be found close to Brno in the southeast of the Czech Republic. It is an area distinguished by distinctive geological formations, underground caverns, and scenic splendor. An outline of the Moravian Karst is given below:

The most well-known and frequently visited caverns in the Moravian Karst are the Punkva caverns. With stalactites, stalagmites, and underground rivers, they provide a captivating underground experience. The Macocha Abyss, a deep sinkhole that reaches a depth of 138 meters, is one of the attractions.

**Sloup-ovka Caves:** The Sloup-ovka Caves are a prominent cave system in the Moravian Karst. These caverns are well-known for their stunning dripstone formations and lakes beneath the surface. Visitors can take guided excursions to explore the fantastical underground environment and discover the geological processes that gave rise to these formations.

**Balcarka Cave:** In the Moravian Karst, there is a smaller but no less remarkable cave known as Balcarka Cave. It is renowned for its distinctive stalactite, stalagmite, and flowstone formations as dripstone embellishments. There is a beautiful underground stream in the cave as well.

**Macocha Gorge**: Located in the Moravian Karst, the Macocha Gorge is a spectacular natural beauty. It is a large sinkhole that was left behind when a network of underground caves collapsed. Visitors can take a boat trip on the underground river or enjoy breathtaking views from the viewpoints as the valley is bordered by towering limestone cliffs.

**Hiking and nature paths**: The Moravian Karst has many hiking and nature trails that let tourists enjoy the area's many landscapes and natural beauties. These routes offer chances to see unusual flora and fauna as they wind through forests, meadows, and rocky formations.

The Moravian Karst is preserved as a nature reserve to maintain its unique ecological values. Numerous different plant and animal species, including rare bats, can be found in the reserve. Visitors can take part in educational events and activities while learning about the region's ecological importance.

**Outdoor Activities**: For those looking for adventure, the Moravian Karst provides a variety of outdoor activities. These activities include horseback riding, cycling, and rock climbing. The area's untamed landscape and breathtaking views provide the ideal setting for outdoor adventure.

The Moravian Karst is a magnificent location that displays both the allure of karst landscapes and the fascinating underground world of caves. It provides a special chance to explore geological marvels and lose oneself in the beauty of nature.

# 10 EVENT AND FESTIVAL

## 10a. MotoGP Brno Grand Prix

The Masaryk Circuit in Brno, Czech Republic, hosts the annual MotoGP Brno, usually referred to as the Brno Grand Prix. It is a part of the coveted MotoGP World Championship, which draws fans of motorsport from all over the world. An overview of the Brno Grand Prix is provided below:

The MotoGP World Championship, which features the best riders and manufacturers in the world, is the top motorcycle racing series. One of the most eagerly anticipated races on the MotoGP schedule is the Brno Grand Prix.

**Masaryk Circuit**: The Brno Grand Prix is held at the Masaryk Circuit. It is a well-known, historically significant motorsports complex that hosts numerous races all year long. The course is renowned for its difficult design, which combines quick straightaways with tricky parts to produce thrilling racing action.

**Race Weekend:** The Brno Grand Prix is held during a race weekend, which usually takes place in August. Practice sessions, qualifying rounds, and the main races in several categories, such as MotoGP, Moto2, and Moto3, are all part of the event.

**MotoGP Racing:** The most powerful and technologically advanced motorcycles compete in the MotoGP class. The event features furious overtaking techniques at high speeds as well as spectacular rider fights. Motorcycle racing fans should not miss the Brno Grand Prix since it draws elite riders and teams.

**Supporting Races**: In addition to the MotoGP races, the Brno Grand Prix frequently hosts Moto2 and Moto3 supporting races. These competitions offer thrilling competition in their respective classifications while showcasing up-and-coming talent.

**Fan Experience:** The Brno Grand Prix provides amazing possibilities for fans to get up close and personal with the action. Views of the circuit are superb from many of the grandstands where spectators may watch the races. Additionally, there are fan zones, autograph sessions, and entertainment options for attendees of all ages at the event.

**Local Culture:** The Brno Grand Prix offers the chance to encounter regional Czech culture. Visitors can savor regional cuisine and drinks from the Czech Republic, take in the lively environment, and socialize with other international motorsport fans.

The Brno Grand Prix is an exhilarating motorsport race that combines fast racing, competitive intensity, and the thrill of the MotoGP World Championship. The Brno Grand Prix delivers an unforgettable weekend of racing action in the heart of the Czech Republic, whether you are an avid motorsports enthusiast or simply searching for an adrenaline experience.

### 10b. Competition for Ignis Brunensis Fireworks

An annual international fireworks competition called the Ignis Brunensis Fireworks Competition takes place in Brno, Czech Republic. The event draws pyrotechnic teams from all over the world and is one of the biggest and most famous pyrotechnics competitions in Europe. The Ignis Brunensis Fireworks Competition is described in the following manner:

The Ignis Brunensis Fireworks Competition was first held as part of the celebrations at the Brno Exhibition Center in 1998, and it has a long and illustrious history. Since then, it has gained popularity and elevated to the top of Brno's list of summer activities.

**Location:** The tournament is held at the breathtaking Brno Reservoir, which serves as a lovely background for the spellbinding fireworks displays. People can assemble to see the performance along the reservoir's banks.

**International Participation**: Renowned pyrotechnic teams from several nations participate in the tournament, demonstrating their technical prowess and creativity in creating beautiful fireworks displays. Each competing team puts on a distinctive pyrotechnic show as they compete to put on the best fireworks display.

The synchronization of the explosions with music is one of the attractions of the Ignis Brunensis Explosions Competition. The pyrotechnic teams coordinate their displays to music, whether it be contemporary music or classical works, producing an enthralling audio-visual spectacle.

A broad variety of pyrotechnic effects, colors, and patterns are used in the fireworks shows, which are renowned for their grandeur and creativity. The displays use a variety of fireworks, including airborne shells, ground-based effects, and sky-illuminating special effects.

Multiple Shows: Over the several days that make up the Ignis Brunensis Fireworks Competition, a different pyrotechnic team will perform each evening. This enables attendees to take in a variety of fireworks displays throughout the event, each with a distinctive theme and aesthetic.

The festival atmosphere is created by the competition, which has food vendors, live music, and other attractions for guests to enjoy. Locals, families, and friends assemble to take in the spectacular displays and spend an unforgettable evening by the reservoir.

The top pyrotechnic team is named and recognized at the competition's grand finale, which concludes the Ignis Brunensis Fireworks Competition. The winning team's artistry and technical mastery are typically displayed in a grand finale performance.

A thrilling event that blends creativity, music, and pyrotechnic expertise is the Ignis Brunensis Fireworks Competition. For viewers of all ages, it is an exhilarating experience that leaves them with lifelong memories of the magnificent fireworks that light up the night sky over the beautiful Brno Reservoir.

## 10c. Shakespeare Festival in the Summer

The Summer Shakespeare Festival is a yearly cultural celebration of William Shakespeare's works that takes place in Brno, Czech Republic. It honors the classic works of the illustrious English playwright by bringing them to life on stage in a distinctive and enthralling manner. A summary of the Summer Shakespeare Festival is provided below:

The Summer Shakespeare Festival was first held in 1995, therefore it has a lengthy history. It has grown to be one of the most well-known cultural occasions in Brno, drawing theater fans from all around the nation and abroad.

**Open-Air Performances**: The festival stages the Shakespearean plays in Brno's picturesque outdoor settings, including castle courtyards, gardens, and parks. The audience can enjoy the plays in a distinctive and natural setting thanks to the open-air presentations, which create a wonderful mood.

**Variety of Productions:** Shakespeare's plays from comedies to tragedies to historical dramas are performed during the festival. Each year, many performances and adaptations are on display, starring great actors and directors who give the classic works their unique perspective.

**High-quality Performances**: The Summer Shakespeare Festival is renowned for its excellent production values, featuring seasoned theater companies and talented actors. Excellent acting, compelling set design, and imaginative storytelling define the performances.

**Multilingual Approach**: Although the plays are usually presented in Czech, some productions include bilingual or English-subtitled performances as well as other multilingualism-related features. This makes it possible for local and international audiences to interact with Shakespeare's works.

**Seminars & Events**: In addition to the plays, the Summer Shakespeare Festival also hosts lectures, seminars, and other theatrical and Shakespeare-related events. Theater fans have the chance to expand their knowledge of and passion for Shakespearean drama through these activities.

**Cultural Exchange**: The event draws theater companies and artists from around the world, promoting cross-cultural dialogue and cooperation. It offers a venue for artists from various nations to assemble and present their interpretations of Shakespeare's works.

Shakespeare's timeless plays are brought to life in a stunning outdoor setting at the Summer Shakespeare Festival in Brno, which is a vivacious celebration of Shakespearean drama. It gives a distinctive cultural encounter and a chance to become engrossed in Shakespeare's plays' allure.

### 10d. **Brno Christmas Markets**

An amazing and joyous environment is created in the city of Brno by the yearly Christmas Markets, which are a much-loved tradition. The Brno Christmas Markets are described in the following manner:

**Námst Svobody:** The center of the Brno Christmas Markets is the city's main square, Námst Svobody. It becomes a winter wonderland, complete with lights, festive booths, and magnificently decorated Christmas trees.

**Handcrafted Gifts and Souvenirs:** A large variety of handcrafted gifts and mementos are available at the markets, including customary Czech ornaments, wooden toys, original jewelry, ceramics, and fabrics. It's the ideal location to find special and heartfelt gifts for loved ones.

**Local Cuisine**: The Christmas Markets are renowned for their delectable fare and beverages. Visitors can savor typical Czech foods including roasted chestnuts, gingerbread cookies, trdelnik (a sweet pastry), and vánoka (a braided Christmas bread). Svaák, or hot mulled wine, is a well-liked libation that warms guests in the chilly winter months.

**Festive mood:** With live music performances, carol singers, and entertainment for all ages, the markets create a happy and festive mood. Visitors can take in the sounds of Christmas carols, take part in seasonal events, and get into the holiday spirit.

Christmas Markets in Brno are decked out in gorgeous decorations and sparkling lights, which creates a lovely atmosphere. Warmth and happiness are evoked by the festive lighting and the smells of traditional foods.

**Ice Rink:** Visitors can lace up their skates and have some wintertime fun on the ice rink that is frequently found at Christmas Markets. Skating in front of the sparkling lights enhances the holiday atmosphere and provides a distinctive activity for groups of friends and family.

**Cultural acts:** A variety of cultural acts, including choirs, dance ensembles, and theatrical productions, are presented at the Christmas Markets. Visitors of all ages can enjoy these acts, which enhance the festive ambiance.

A lovely way to spend the holiday season is to visit the Christmas Markets in Brno, which feature a variety of traditional crafts from the Czech Republic, delectable foods, and festive entertainment. The Christmas Markets in Brno are a must-see during the winter months, whether you're looking for one-of-a-kind presents, delectable food, or just want to take in the magical ambiance.

# 11 PRACTICAL INFORMATION

## 11a. Lodging Options

There are numerous lodging alternatives in Brno to accommodate diverse tastes and price ranges. Here are some typical accommodations you might want to take into account:

**Hotels:** A variety of hotels are available in Brno, ranging from five-star hotels to more affordable alternatives. Hotels offer welcoming accommodations, conveniences like bars, restaurants, and fitness centers, as well as frequently available extras like room service and a concierge.

**Guesthouses and Bed & Breakfasts:** These accommodations offer a cozier, more intimate setting. They often have fewer rooms and provide a more individualized experience. These lodgings are frequently managed by families and offer a cozy setting with breakfast.

**Apartments and holiday rentals:** For individuals looking for more room and solitude, renting an apartment or a vacation home can be a terrific option. You can prepare your meals in these fully furnished, kitchen-equipped rooms, giving you greater freedom and independence throughout your stay. They are perfect for families or tourists who want to stay for a longer period.

**Hostels**: If you're on a tight budget or prefer a more sociable setting, hostels may be a good option for you. Various hostels in Brno provide individual rooms or shared dormitory-style accommodations at reasonable prices. Along with common areas where you can meet other travelers, hostels may provide services like shared kitchens and laundry rooms.

Brno also provides boutique hotels and design hotels for those looking for a distinctive and fashionable lodging experience. These places frequently have cutting-edge architecture, creative interior design, and a focus on offering guests an exceptional and unforgettable experience.

**Campgrounds:** There are campgrounds in and near Brno if you like to camp or have a camper van. These parks offer services including restrooms, tent and RV campsites, and occasionally recreational features like playgrounds or swimming pools.

When selecting a place to stay, take into account things like location, accessibility to facilities and public transit, amenities and services offered, and your budget. To guarantee availability and lock in the best prices, it is advised to make reservations in advance, especially during busy travel times.

### 11b. Public Transportation:

The public transportation network in Brno is well-developed and offers easy and effective ways to navigate the city. Some significant elements of Brno's public transit are as follows:

In Brno, trams are a well-liked method of transportation. The majority of the city is covered by the tram network, making it simple to get to different areas and attractions. From early in the morning until late at night, trams run, with frequent service throughout rush hour.

Buses: To complement its tram system, Brno also has a robust bus network. Buses provide communication to the city's periphery and serve places that trams do not reach. They run on a similar timetable to trams and offer continuous service.

Tickets and Fees: A valid ticket must be purchased to ride the public transportation system in Brno. At selected bus stations, convenience stores, and tram stops, ticket machines are available for the purchase of tickets. There are available single-ride tickets, day passes, and longer-term passes (like weekly or monthly tickcts). Before boarding the tram or bus, don't forget to validate your ticket.

Integrated Ticketing System: In Brno, a single ticket may be used for both buses and trams within a predetermined time frame thanks to the city's integrated ticketing system. This makes switching between several public transit options simple.

Information & Timetables: The official website of the Brno Public Transport Company (DPMB) contains comprehensive information about public transportation routes, timetables, and costs. At tram and bus stops, you can also find timetables and route maps. Real-time information on bus and tram arrivals is additionally provided via several mobile apps and websites.

Accessibility: People with mobility impairments can use the public transportation system in Brno. To make boarding easier for passengers in wheelchairs or pushing strollers, trams, and buses are fitted with ramps or low-floor doors.

**11c. Centers for Tourist Information:**

The city's tourist information offices can provide you with useful advice and assistance while you are in Brno. These facilities are provided with competent people who can offer advice, maps, brochures, and suggestions to make your visit more enjoyable. Here are a few Brno tourist information offices:

Radnická 8 is home to the tourist information center, which provides a variety of services and resources, including maps, guides, and details on nearby landmarks, activities, and transportation.

The Panenská 1 location of the Brno Tourist Information Center offers a wide range of tourist services, including multilingual staff, travel suggestions, lodging advice, and help with making tour or ticket reservations.

If you are flying into Brno, there is a tourist information center at Brno-Turany Airport that you can visit. The center provides advice on attractions and services in the city as well as information on transportation and airport-related matters.

These tourist information centers are great places to find current information on Brno, including suggestions for places to visit, cultural events, and useful travel tips. Additionally, they can offer assistance with hotel reservations, city maps, and recommendations for places to eat, shop, and have fun.

## Useful Words and Phrases

Basic Salutations

Hello: Ahoj
Happy morning: Good luck roo
Salutations: Dobré odpoledne
Good night: Brrr veer
Goodbye: Na shledanou Kind regards: Děkuji
Please: Pros I'm sorry: Promising to Request Information:

Where are you: Kde je?

Can you assist me? Could you help me?

I'm unsure: jsem se ztratil(a)

What is the price? : To what extent?

You can speak English, right? Do you love English?

Getting Snacks and Drinks:

I'd like to... "Chtl(a) bych,"

What would you suggest? How do you proceed?

Please pass the money: et, prosm Salutations: No problem!

Transportation:

Which bus/tram stop is it? Where is the bus/tram station?

How can I get there? How do you do...?

Is this seat occupied? I want to sedate you.

How far is it from here? Is this an old odtud?

Shopping:

Kolik to stoj? : How much is this?

Should I try it on? Do you think that's right?

Do you have an expanded/reduced size? Do you possess velikost?

Emergencies:

Pomoc, help!

A doctor is needed: Pot'ebuji dr./dr.ku

Where is the closest medical facility? Where is the nearest nemocnic?

Zavolejte poliicii, call the cops!

Whenever you deal with locals, keep in mind to be courteous and considerate. Even if you don't speak Czech well, learning a few fundamental phrases can help you interact with locals and demonstrate your respect for their way of life.

**Tourist Information Centers**: As previously indicated, free city maps, guides, and brochures are available at the tourist information centers in Brno, including the Radnická and Panenská locations. These sources provide useful details about attractions, travel, events, and other topics.

Digital versions of city maps and guides are available on the official website of Brno as well as the websites of regional tourism organizations. These websites offer in-depth details about the city's attractions, events, lodging choices, food alternatives, and more.

You can navigate Brno's streets, find hidden jewels, and make the most of your time in the city by following this guide book. You can explore Brno with confidence if you have access to trustworthy information, whether you prefer printed or digital alternatives.

Printed in Great Britain
by Amazon

40595877R00106